LIVE FREE

LIVE FREE

Exceed Your Highest Expectations

DeVon Franklin

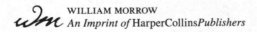

WILLIAM MORROW
An Imprint of HarperCollins*Publishers*

HarperCollins books may be purchased for educational, business, or sales promotional use. For information, please email the Special Markets Department at SPsales@harpercollins.com.

FIRST EDITION

Designed by Bonni Leon-Berman

Library of Congress Cataloging-in-Publication Data has been applied for.

ISBN 978-0-06-303117-3

21 22 23 24 25   LSC   10 9 8 7 6 5 4 3 2 1

To every caged bird . . . it's your time to break free

CONTENTS

LIVE FREE

INTRODUCTION

Are You Living Free?

> When I discover who I am, I will be free.
> —Ralph Ellison

> You wanna fly, you got to give up the shit that weighs you down.
> —Toni Morrison

As I write this, in the summer of 2020, we are in the middle of a pandemic. Isolation, loneliness, and despair are exploding. Our lives have forever been impacted in ways beyond our control. Jobs, businesses, homes, lives, and livelihoods are being lost. At the same time, there's a groundswell against the systemic racism and inequality at the foundation of our country. Tensions are at a fever pitch as this call for greater compassion and equity grows to a deafening level. The obvious paths forward have been interrupted. Debts are rising. Disappointments are mounting. Hope is waning. We are losing our sense of self and where we fit in the world. Dreams are dashed. Hearts are troubled. This is not what we *expected*.

And yet, these issues are not completely new. Our current troubles are only exacerbating what we were already feeling—anxious, exhausted, stressed, and disconnected from ourselves and the people we care about the most. Before our normal lives were halted, most of us were doing too much, and paying for it, as we tried to live up to the cultural ideal that everybody should be grinding. Then, we felt like we *had* to be too busy in order to be successful. Now, we're caught somewhere in the middle, unsure where to go from here, or how to rebuild.

You may be wondering: *How do I survive? How do I make it through? How do I live the life I feel destined to live, in the face of so many factors seemingly out of my control?* You are not alone; I've pondered the exact same questions. I've sought answers, in the name of greater personal freedom and happiness, and I've made some startling discoveries. Even before the pandemic began, I had a realization about the key to getting the most out of life, and now, as our world has been turned upside down, this discovery has proven even more urgent.

Here's what I have come to know: **unmanaged expectations lead to an unhappy life.**

This is the true secret that no one is talking about. One of the reasons why we have so much difficulty isn't life itself—it's what we have expected from life up until now, and how upset we have been when our expectations did not come to pass.

The people who seek advice from me almost always complain about how miserable they are because of something that hasn't happened yet. That's one of the main problems with expectations: they keep us from living in the present, enjoying the process, and appreciating what we do have. Instead, we obsess over what we don't have. We're too busy focusing on what we expect to receive, whether it has any basis in reality or not. Or we're too hung up on the pain of past disappointment.

Our focus goes to where it shouldn't be—on other people and situations outside of ourselves. That distracts us from taking full accountability for our own choices and contentment. Instead of maximizing the time that does exist (the present), we outsource our happiness, satisfaction, and peace to a time that doesn't yet exist (the future): *Oh, when I get this job*, or, *When this promotion happens*, or, *When I get married . . . then I'll be happy.* News flash: if you're not happy now, you won't be happy then.

THE EXPECTATION REVELATION

You may not even be aware that you're not reacting to the actual events of your life. Instead, you're reacting to your expectations of what you thought should've happened, what didn't happen, or what could've happened. Let's be honest—if this is you (and hey, I was guilty of this too), then here's a hard truth. As of right now, you aren't in control . . . your expectations are running your life. Maybe even ruining your life.

Gallup's annual "Global Emotions" report for 2019 once again found America to be among the most stressed-out countries in the world: 55 percent of those polled had felt stressed out during the day, and the global average was still high at 35 percent. (And this was *before* the pandemic!)

How many people's lives have been misspent or wasted because they're living according to the expectations of their parents, their friends, their church, their spouse, or anyone else, instead of what they feel called to do in their heart? Too many. Maybe you know deep down, as you read this, that you've fallen into this trap too. Don't worry; I'm here to help you. By the time you finish this book, you will be living according to the life you've been called to live—not the expectations anyone else has put on you.

For me, it all came into focus when I examined my own life and the areas in which I sometimes struggled, and asked myself if my expectations were contributing to my unhappiness. I looked at anywhere I was experiencing some discontent, such as certain aspects of my career, certain areas of my marriage, or personal goals I hadn't achieved yet. I asked myself the question: *What is the source of my unhappiness?* This analysis was incredibly powerful—it was like sliding on a pair of glasses. I immediately realized I was being burdened by extraneous expectations, and I wasn't even aware of many of them. As I reflected on all of this, I understood it wasn't an issue of me not doing enough, or not being good enough, or not receiving enough. My expectations— of myself, of other people, of circumstances, of situations—were not managed or set. And so, my expectations were weighing me down.

Next, I applied this lens to the people who'd been coming to me for help with their lives and careers. I saw that they had unrealistic ideas about that promotion they wanted, or about how their hard work would be rewarded in comparison to their peers. Or they'd been dating someone for years, and they had the unrealistic idea about this person changing. Their disappointment when these things didn't come to pass as they'd hoped was eating them up inside—it was preventing them from seeing the aspects of their life they did like and could control.

And then I looked around me at our country, and why we're in the shape we're in. Maybe we haven't set our expectations properly. By that I don't mean that we shouldn't rely on certain protections and assistance from our government. We should—but sometimes when we have an expectation, we may absolve ourselves of the responsibility to make sure it gets done. Maybe we need to stop automatically expecting our elected officials to do their jobs. Instead, we must hold them accountable and become the change we want to see.

ARE YOU LIVING FREE?

Living free—isn't that what we all want, really? To be free. Free from the burdens and stress of trying to live up to, or down to, what others expect from us. Free from the prison of negative thoughts and self-talk that keeps us feeling trapped. Free from the anxiety that we aren't going to succeed. For you, living free may seem so far from your current reality that you're not sure it's even possible, or what it could entail, for that matter.

**TO LIVE FREE MEANS YOU ARE NOT UNDER
THE MENTAL, PHYSICAL, OR EMOTIONAL
CONTROL OF ANYONE OR ANYTHING.
YOU LIVE ACCORDING TO
THE EXPECTATIONS YOU CHOOSE.**

For too long, you've been giving your power away to people, circumstances, and situations. It's time to take your power back, which you do by making the commitment to live free.

Living free is about taking on fewer burdens; having fewer obstacles that block your joy; thinking clearly; feeling happier; worrying a lot less (or not at all) about what other people think of you; and being fully content to be yourself (not who everyone expects you to be).

Of course, for each individual, freedom will be a different experience. You get to define what living free looks like for you, and it is always a wonderful blessing when you do. Now that I've given you a taste of the greater freedom that's waiting for you, imagine for yourself:

- How would it feel if I were really free?
- Would my life be anything like the one I am living today?
- Who would I be if I chose to be my true self?

Well, prepare to live out your answers to these questions, starting right now. To live free, you need to cast off as many expectations as possible and to set those that remain. This process will help you become crystal clear on your expectations and better at managing them properly. You will see a tremendous improvement in all areas of your life.

After assessing and possibly letting go of the illusions and false goals that have been contributing to your dissatisfaction, you can properly set your expectations and live more in a time of less. Setting expectations simply requires asking yourself two critical questions, which you'll learn more about in the pages that follow:

- Is it a realistic or unrealistic expectation?
- Is it a spoken or unspoken expectation?

I will teach you how to understand what's realistic versus unrealistic, and what's the difference between a spoken and an unspoken request. Yes, this process will require some tough conversations with yourself, and quite possibly with the people closest to you. But the benefits are immediate and great.

This journey will help you become clear about who you really are (not who you're expected to be), what you really value, and what you truly want out of your life, which will allow you to live the life you actually choose for yourself, in the here and now.

As I've applied these truths in my own life, they have made a radical difference in my stress level, happiness, and overall disposition. They've helped me become more flexible and accepting of changes in my life that previously would have been upsetting.

I've discovered that once your expectations are set properly, the stage is set for the life you've always wanted—and deserved. My deepest prayer is that this book will be very healing for you. I pray it will lead you toward a freer, more contented, more grateful you. And not in some far-off future, but right here and now, right inside of you, where your happiness has been waiting for you all along.

SET YOURSELF FREE

There are four main areas in your life where expectations come into play:

- **PERSONAL:** Your expectations of yourself
- **CULTURAL:** Your expectations of your culture and the culture's expectations of you
- **RELATIONAL:** Your expectations of others and others' expectations of you
- **PROFESSIONAL:** Your expectations of your career and your job's expectations of you

To live more freely, you'll have to gain control in all of these areas. To do so, you must evaluate each and every one of your expectations and determine where it came from. If it doesn't serve you, you must let it go. By doing so, you will release yourself from its grip. Do this again, and again, and again, until you're left with only the expectations of your choosing. Then, any expectations you do keep must be set carefully; make sure these expectations are realistic and communicate them to anyone else who might need to agree to meet them. Then and only then will your expectations be set properly.

This, right here, is the secret to a happier life! And it works.

The problem is, if we've never stopped to analyze where our expectations come from, or how they've been playing out in our lives, they have probably led us to make some compromised choices. Possibly for the first time ever you will get real with yourself by asking:

- Is my job the one I really wanted?
- Is this relationship the right one?
- Do I live where I really want to live?
- Honestly, is this the life I truly want to be living?

This can be difficult. If you have the courage to be truthful with yourself, the answers to these questions can be extremely painful. As can the recognition that you could be living in ways you don't really like or value, trying to make someone else happy, or trying to live up to some version of yourself that is far different than who God created you to be. You might find yourself realizing: *Oh, no, this is not where I want to be, who I want to be, how I want to be living.*

Once I began understanding the true impact of expectations, it rocked me to my core and brought me to tears. There was so much in my life I'd expected to happen that didn't; I'd expected so many things from other people that I shouldn't have expected. Can you relate? I reached the point where I had to ask myself a question, which I want you to ask yourself now: *If this isn't the life of my conscious choosing, how do I find one that is?*

If you can't answer that question right away, don't be discouraged—that's what the work in this book is meant to help you discover. There is so much more contentment waiting for you. By finally setting your own expectations and shedding the rest, your life will open up. You really do create your own happiness, and if you try to outsource it to anyone or anything else, you will always be dissatisfied.

Setting your expectations for yourself is a whole new approach to life, one that allows you to be more carefree and less burdened. Through the examples and exercises in these pages, you'll learn how to do this for yourself. In the end, you'll be more grateful for what you have. You'll possess more hope. You'll have reassessed what's important to you, and your reality will be rebuilt, better than ever before.

It's time to live free. Are you ready?

Part I

PERSONAL EXPECTATIONS

1

THE DANGERS OF EXPECTATIONS

You are your own worst enemy. If you can learn to stop expecting impossible perfection, in yourself and others, you may find the happiness that has always eluded you.
—LISA KLEYPAS

Expectations were like fine pottery. The harder you held them, the more likely they were to crack.
—BRANDON SANDERSON

Expectations are weights. They can weigh us down physically. They can weigh us down mentally. They can weigh us down spiritually. They put our focus too much on where it shouldn't be—on the past, on the future, and on other people—and distract us from accepting accountability for our own happiness and choices, in the here and now. When we take on too many of them, they make our lives harder—and can actually push our goals further away.

Too many expectations can crush you. That's why they can be so dangerous. Before you can fly, you've got to shed; part of the process of setting expectations is letting go of many of those you've taken on throughout your life, including those you were unaware of up until now.

In this section, we're going to open by discussing personal expectations, how and why they can be detrimental, and all of the powerful shifts you can make in your life by properly setting them. But before we get into the nitty-gritty of the process, let's examine their origins. According to Ben Silliman, family life specialist at the University of Wyoming Cooperative Extension Service, we usually pick up our expectations unintentionally, unconsciously, and most often in our childhood. This is why it's so important to stop and identify our expectations and where they originated. He points to three main sources:

- **FAMILY**: Parent/grandparent models, attitudes among relatives, siblings
- **SOCIETY**: Friends, neighborhood, school/church, TV/media
- **PERSONAL EXPERIENCES AND PREFERENCES**: Hurts, events, and hopes

To Silliman's list I would add our career or professional life as a potential source of the expectations we carry. Each of these sources influences us to different degrees. But we all have taken on the expectations of our race, gender, economic status, religious background, family, social group, or workplace, to name a few.

There's a lot of pressure that comes from identifying with certain groups and their expectations, which can range from what we're supposed to wear to where we're supposed to go, the music we're supposed to listen to, and the core foundations of who we are, such as the beliefs we're supposed to hold or the ways we're supposed to behave.

This would be pressure enough if each of us identified with only one group, but most of us fall into several different ones, all of which come with their own expectations. For example, I'm a Black man, a Christian, a son, a brother, a husband, and a friend. I'm an author. I'm a Hollywood producer. I'm in the public eye. Believe me, I know how many expectations these various roles can put upon a single person. I am well aware that many people believe I'm supposed to think and act as they feel I should, based on the groups with which I identify.

Here's the rub: if you or I don't live up to certain expectations, we're going to be vilified, judged, and probably shunned—not for holding any beliefs that are negative, or in any way despicable, but for having beliefs that may not line up with what some people within our various groups believe. So we often, without realizing it, conform to what's expected of us, even if it's not what we want to do, out of fear of what will happen if we don't. How can this possibly be a sane way to live? It's not. It can be overwhelming, demoralizing, draining, and downright disruptive to our well-being. And yet, for most of us, this is how it's always been.

Have you ever stopped to think about what expectations are being put on you by others or by the groups you identify with? If you have never thought about this, now is the time.

For example, if you're a man, you're supposed to think this way. If you're a woman, you're supposed to think that way. If you're religious, you're supposed to do this, but not that. If you're young, you're supposed to like this. If you're successful, you're supposed to drive this car. If you're a social media influencer, you're supposed to have this number of followers. Sound familiar? There is a significant cost to unconsciously conforming to such expectations.

I know I've conformed to what's been expected of me before, and I resented it. You may be doing it right now. But I ask you: Is it worth it? Going along with what's expected, rather than standing up for your right to live as you see fit, and how God has ordained for you to live, might seem easier in the moment, but it comes with a heavy price. We cannot do this long-term without suffering negative effects—from resentment on one end to self-destructive behaviors on the other.

It can affect anyone and everyone. As pop music sensation Demi Lovato has publicly expressed in interviews, the pressure she felt to maintain a certain level of physical perfection was so intense that it eventually compelled her to act out in a very dangerous way. Her unhappiness became so great that it caused her to accidentally overdose after six years of sobriety. As she described her life on *The Ellen Show* in March 2020, others controlled every aspect of her behavior, but the rules were particularly strict around food, especially before photo shoots. She felt powerless and miserable. Plus, she was given no support for the eating disorder with which she was already struggling. After all, being a certain shape was one of the expectations that came along with her role as a pop star. This perfect storm of anxiety and misery eventually became too much for her:

> I lived a life for the past six years that I felt like wasn't my own. . . . My life, I just felt, was so—and I hate to use this word—but I feel like it was controlled by so many people around me. . . . I was stuck in this unhappy position. Here I am sober, and I'm thinking to myself, "I'm six years sober, but I'm miserable. I'm even more miserable than I was when I was drinking. Why am I sober?"

When Lovato first tried to warn her team that she was in danger of relapsing, she was told that she was "being very selfish," that she "would ruin things, not just for you, but for us as well." So not only did she feel like she had no healthier path to freedom, but she also felt abandoned, which activated her childhood trauma, contributing to her decision to use again. Following her first relapse, she came clean in her 2018 song "Sober." A month after it was released, she had an even more serious episode: she was found unconscious in her home and treated with Narcan, which is typically used in cases of opioid overdoses. She was rushed to the hospital and required to stay there for several days, until her condition stabilized enough for her to seek addiction treatment.

When Lovato thankfully survived her ordeal and emerged from three months at a live-in rehab facility, she was clear that the changes she needed to make in her life went far beyond addressing her addiction and eating disorder. She fired her management team and hired a new manager—someone who, as she said in an interview with *Bustle* magazine, supported her desire to put the focus back on her music, not on her body.

I applaud Demi for her courage, not only to seek the treatment she needed but also to release herself from the unhealthy expectations of others. She came to realize they didn't match who she wanted to be. She took control of setting her own expectations—about her body, her artistry, and her happiness—and her life is now better for it.

I applaud you, in advance, for your courage in committing to do this work. Are there unhealthy habits you've taken on? I guarantee they are probably related to the pressures you are feeling from an expectation you don't want to or feel you can't meet. As long as you only try to change the behavior, without looking at what lies beneath it, you will have a hard time healing yourself. In fact, you may conquer one bad habit only to take up another. That's exactly how detrimental it can be to live with the burden of others' expectations.

Ask yourself:

- What unhealthy habits have been keeping me from living my best life?

- Am I acting out in this way because I feel pressure to live up to my own, or someone else's, unrealistic expectations?
- Has the pressure of these expectations caused me to retreat into a fantasy about my future, rather than putting my focus on what I have and can achieve in the here and now?
- What steps can I take to release these expectations and be healthier and more present?

We have to give ourselves permission to be free—letting go of any and all expectations that we did not set for ourselves and do not agree with and instead allowing ourselves to think and live how we choose, not how others have chosen for us to live. We also have to allow ourselves to be imperfect. At whatever stage of our journey we're on, finding unconditional self-love and acceptance is the first step toward the confidence that will allow us to be our best selves.

WHAT ARE EXPECTATIONS?

Before we go any further, let's define expectations:

**EXPECTATIONS ARE STRONG BELIEFS
ABOUT WHAT SHOULD HAPPEN.**

Let's break down that idea even more. A belief is defined as an acceptance that something is true, even if it isn't based on fact or evidence. Beliefs, which may feel as real as concrete, are central to who we are. They are ideas we are willing to live by or die for. But our beliefs can sometimes cause us to misjudge what is happening, or will happen, by leading us to misinterpret certain facts in our life. They can cause us to jump to illogical conclusions about how we think situations should play out, when we may not have the right information to back this up.

The first step is to break free from the grip of limiting beliefs. To do so, we have to first understand where they come from and how they function. It's critical to identify the sources of beliefs and, most importantly, to break down why they can be so dangerous.

We are going to rethink our understanding of expectations, and I'll warn you now, this could be difficult. It might go against how you've always been taught to think about who you are and how you should live. But it's an absolutely crucial step in the path toward living free.

BELIEFS TAKE THE FORM OF ASSUMPTIONS, STANDARDS, JUDGMENTS, AND PROJECTIONS.

Let's look at the potential danger posed by each form of expectation.

Beware of False Assumptions

> *An assumption is "a thing that is accepted as true or as certain to happen, without proof."*
> —OXFORD ENGLISH DICTIONARY

Our assumptions are the first way beliefs can manifest themselves. *Without proof*—that's the important part of the definition. We assume that our belief is certain to come to pass, even though we have no real evidence to support that assumption. For example, let's say you've assumed that if you pay the high cost of tuition for a prestigious college, your dream job will be waiting for you when you graduate. So, even if this school isn't really your ideal choice, you decide to attend anyway, certain that the ends will justify the means. However, unless someone offers you a position when you enroll in that school, you're potentially making a false assumption. There is no guarantee the school will deliver on the promise you've attached to it.

Now you may be saying, "Yeah, there's no guarantee, but it's highly likely." I would challenge you: "Highly likely" based on what? As the finance gurus caution when you're investing, past performance is no indicator of future results. The issue isn't your decision to attend the school; the issue is basing that decision on the assumption you will then be hired in the job you want when you graduate. There are so many other factors at play.

This example can be applied to any area of your life. Why is it important to examine your assumptions? If you're not aware of them, you might be devastated if your assumed outcome doesn't come to pass.

It's far easier than you may realize to make a false assumption.

A FALSE ASSUMPTION IS TREATING A POSSIBILITY AS A CERTAINTY.

It's not a stretch to base your whole existence on a false assumption— for instance, that what you study, whom you marry, or where you live will *guarantee* you the happiness you want. All of these factors may possibly increase your happiness, but there is no assurance that they will. If you have been treating possibilities as certainties, it can be difficult (but not impossible) to course-correct. The earlier you can catch a false assumption, the easier it will be to pivot to a more proactive, productive direction and stop courting a potential fantasy.

There may be many false assumptions running your life. Ask yourself right now:

- What are the critical assumptions I'm making about my future?
- How many of these assumptions are false?

When you begin examining all of this, it takes courage to stop basing your life on any false assumptions you discover, no matter how significant. But the benefits are immediate, and the process becomes easier with practice.

When you start eliminating false assumptions, you'll experience incredible clarity. It's like praying without worrying about the outcome. Instead of saying, *My desired outcome must happen in the way I want it to or I'll be devastated,* you will say, *It would be great to have my desired outcome, but if that's not what happens, that's okay. I didn't make this decision assuming it would.* Your clarity will improve once you start getting real with yourself about the foundation of your life choices and, if they're not grounded in reality, rethinking them.

Who Sets the Standards?

A standard is "a level of quality or achievement used for judging someone or something."
—MACMILLAN DICTIONARY

There's nothing wrong with having standards, high standards even. However, let's talk about the downside. What happens when your beliefs become standards for others? It works like this:

I have an expectation of myself, and as a result,
I've set that expectation as the standard by
which everyone else should live.

Do you believe that everyone in your life should live by your standards? You alone set the standards for yourself, and for nobody else but you. Be careful not to lose perspective and impose your standards on other people, even if you believe them to be realistic. You are not a dictator, and other people have the right to respond and act however they choose. Blindly imposing your standards on other people pre-vents you from seeing them as they actually are and allowing them to have their own path in life. You can also become tremendously frustrated when your standards aren't met.

On the other hand, how do you respond when others measure you against their standards, based on beliefs you don't agree with? If you are anything like me, the answer is, *probably not well*. Don't allow oth-ers to impose the standards they choose to live by on you, and resist the temptation to do the same, by taking on their values as your own. Only you should choose your own standards. Don't give that power to anyone else.

Judge Not, Lest Ye Be Judged

> A judgment is *"the process of forming an opinion or evaluation."*
> —Merriam-Webster Dictionary

If we're not careful, our expectations can make us judgmental. Here's what that looks like:

> *I allow my expectation to become the standard,*
> *and if you don't meet it, I judge you.*

We're seeing this a lot in our culture. As discussed earlier, depend-ing on how you identify and who you identify with, you may be ex-pected to live a certain way or risk getting "canceled" if you don't. For example, in the Christian community this happens all too fre-quently: if you don't meet certain people's expectations for "a good Christian," you will be judged and often vilified.

There are two main reasons why people are judgmental. The first is that they feel so restricted and judged themselves that their mentality becomes, *If I can't live free, then you can't live free.* Or, *If I have to live in this prison of rigid rules, you should too.* Second, judgmental people are often very insecure. They fear they aren't living up to their own expectations or those of others around them, so they take comfort in finding flaws in other people.

Many people may not even be aware that they're feeling confined by certain restrictive beliefs in their community. That's why the message of this book always boils down to doing your work, for yourself, and carefully setting your expectations in all areas of your life. We'll dive deeper into how to do that in later pages, but for starters, we are learning how to release the old ways of being and thinking that don't serve us anymore.

When you find yourself being judgmental, ask yourself:

- Am I living free, or do I feel restricted and/or limited in my life?
- Do I have some insecurities that I need to deal with?

The worst is when people act like they are law enforcement. They make themselves responsible for policing how you and/or other people should behave. We must stop judging others based on our own expectations and biases. And we must stop allowing others to judge or condemn us based on *their* expectations and biases.

Think about how awful it feels to be judged by someone else, especially when they misunderstand you or your intentions. You don't want to be the kind of person who does that to others, do you? And it's not just the people on the receiving end who experience a negative impact. The *Psychology Today* article "Why Judging Others Is Bad for You" by Rubin Khoddam, PhD, explores the high cost of such behavior. One of his central points is that we often misinterpret reality, assuming our judgment is the truth when really it's our opinion. Living our lives based on false ideas about other people and the world is dangerous, and if your expectations are based on such assumptions, they are likely to be unrealistic. Khoddam explains why unrealistic expectations can never be properly set:

> We fuse with our opinions . . . meaning that we can't tell the difference between what our opinion is and what the reality is. And in the end our perception becomes our reality. . . . We end up believing our thoughts/judgments and take our thoughts as facts. We believe that person is horrible. . . . We believe the movie was awful. Instead of seeing our multitude of judgments as a perception . . . we put on situations, we see it as a truth. By doing this we subliminally create a separation and a lack of acceptance of other's beliefs.

This is a timely warning, especially when our country is roiling with unrest, much of it based on the judgments people are making about others, who happen to be of different races, genders, or political affiliations than themselves. Everyone loses when it comes to judging.

Forecasts Aren't the Only Projections

A projection means attributing your ideas, attitudes, or feelings to other people.

The fourth common form that expectations take is projection. A film metaphor is a great way to explain the danger of projection: In a movie theater, you see captivating images onscreen that are so vivid and real-looking that you become caught up in what they're showing you. But if you walk up to that screen, the images aren't really there. They're being *projected*.

I'm reminded of a scene in one of my favorite films, *The Pursuit of Happyness*, which I had the blessing of working on when I was an executive at Sony Pictures Entertainment. Chris Gardner Sr., played by Will Smith, is on the basketball court with his son, Chris Gardner Jr., played by Jaden Smith. Chris Jr. shoots and misses. Chris Sr. grabs the rebound and tells his son not to worry about playing basketball—he could never play himself, so his son won't be very good either. Chris Jr. is hurt and starts packing up to leave the court. After Chris Sr. sees how he demoralized his son, he has an epiphany and says: "Wait, I'm sorry. Don't let anybody ever tell you that you can't do something. You want something, you go after it, period."

See how projection works? We form our ideas about ourselves, or our beliefs about life, and then we impose them on others in potentially damaging ways. This occurs in our everyday lives all of the time.

The most dangerous and potentially damaging projections are usually those that parents foist on their children—"I went to this school, so you should too," or "I got straight As, so you should too." Sometimes parents are trying to relive their youth through their children by having them accomplish things they weren't able to do themselves. "I always wanted to be the captain of the team, so you should try harder at sports." "I wish I had been able to go to college, so academic excellence should be important to you."

A 2018 report by the Robert Wood Johnson Foundation, which was widely covered in publications like the *Washington Post* and the *Los Angeles Times*, said that expectations of high achievement, such as an "excessive pressure to excel," should be added to the list of the top factors that have a negative impact on adolescent wellness in our country. It's right up there with more obvious dangers like poverty, discrimination, and trauma. The potential for damage from this expectation is enormous.

What's so interesting about these two divergent examples—*The Pursuit of Happyness* and the findings of this study—is that they show the danger of any kind of projection, whether positive or negative. If whatever we expect from someone else is based on our own version of reality rather than what's real, we are doing them a great disservice. And we are setting them up for failure. How do you even know what's real? Through observation, not evaluation. In other words, observe what is true without evaluating it based on what you want reality to be.

This is how parents can lose their child. They keep evaluating the child, projecting onto them what they want to be there, which may not ever be, instead of accepting them for who they are and letting them figure out where they fit in the world. For their part, children who don't release these familial expectations that they never asked for or agreed to risk stifling their true selves and never finding their deeper happiness, never truly creating the life they want.

The same potential dangers lurk in all of our relationships and often wreak havoc if we stay unaware of our projections until it's too late. As you've already begun to see, expectations may seem like a simple concept—and they are, at their root. But especially when we haven't set them properly, they can create big, complicated problems in all areas of our lives, warp our perspective, damage our relationships, and leave us generally unhappy.

The time to address these potential pitfalls is now. The last thing we want is to reach the end of our lives and regret that we didn't course-correct, when we had the chance, in order to feel fully at peace with the existence we created for ourselves and our impact during the time we were given.

As pointed out by life coach Evan Dwan in his piece "What if My Whole Life Has Been Wrong?," this was the fate of the character Ivan Ilyich in the well-known Leo Tolstoy story *The Death of Ivan Ilyich*. In order to avoid this same fate, Dwan suggests doing a life review, not on our deathbeds, but right now, when we still have the power to change. I see the work we are doing around expectations as a powerful first step. As Dwan states: "The great gift of this reflection is the realization, if we are unhappy with how we are living, that there is still time to change and start to create a legacy that will allow us to leave this life at peace, when the time comes."

I want you to begin creating a legacy for yourself that goes beyond any material possessions you have acquired or achievements you have made. Nothing you do will have a greater impact on what you leave behind than stopping right now and setting your expectations for yourself.

CHAPTER 1 Expectation Examinations

It's time to identify the expectations that are shaping your life and decide if you agree with them or not. It's the first step in learning how to properly set a few carefully chosen expectations and to let go of all of the rest. Each chapter will close with a handful of these examinations, related to the topics discussed in the chapter.

Clear out some time and space where you can be alone. Designate a journal for this purpose or pull up your digital notepad on your smartphone. Prepare to be honest.

1. What are your top five *personal* expectations of yourself? Once you have listed them, organize them in order of significance or weight, from most to least important.

2. Now that you have made your list, go through it, and ask yourself:
- Which expectations came from me?
- Which expectations came from outside of me—from my family, my community, my church, my school, or a group with which I identify?
- Are there any items on my list that I don't really agree with?
- Are some of these expectations unrealistic?

- Why am I afraid to let go of the expectations I don't agree with, or the ones I now see are unrealistic?

3. When have you projected onto others? Why did you want other people to think or behave in this way? Was it fair of you? Can you release your expectations of them now?

4. Have you been putting others' happiness before your own? If you could stop worrying about what other people think and feel about you and your choices, what are five things you would stop doing? What are five things you would start doing?

2

THE SECRET SOFTWARE RUNNING YOUR LIFE

Expectation is the root of all heartache.

—William Shakespeare

What screws us up the most in life is the picture in our head of what it's supposed to be.

—Jeremy Binns

Your expectations are the secret software running on the hardware of your mind. They control your emotions, decisions, and actions. They distort your perspective. They drive your choices. They influence your feelings about outcomes, often in ways you aren't even aware of. That's the danger: too often you don't realize this is happening. You feel like you are in control, but you aren't—this hidden program is actually in charge.

And here's the kicker: you may not have even coded the program

that's underlying your own life, because many of the expectations
you are living by are ones you didn't consciously choose for yourself.
They were chosen for you by other people, circumstances, and situations.

In order to understand how powerful expectations are in creating
the applications that are currently running your life, we need to first
achieve a deeper understanding of how software works and is created. Dr. David T. Bourgeois gave this definition of software in his
book *Information Systems for Business and Beyond*:

> Software gives the instructions that tell the hardware what
> to do. There are two basic categories of software: *operating
> systems* and *applications*. Operating systems provide access
> to the computer hardware. . . . Application software is de-
> signed to meet a specific goal. Software is developed through
> a process called programming, in which a programmer uses
> a programming language to put together the logic needed to
> create the program.

Every day, software runs our smartphones and computers and,
increasingly, almost every tool on which we rely, from our cars to
our refrigerators. We take it for granted that the apps within these
devices will work without much input from us other than upgrading our operating systems from time to time. When something goes
wrong, we call customer support or replace our devices—fixing or
reprogramming the software would be way beyond the capabilities
of most of us.

But when it comes to our own software, what do we do when
something goes wrong? There's no Genius Bar, Geek Squad, or instant upgrade to fix our problems. If you are upset, bitter, discontented, nonclinically depressed, frustrated, or sad, there's a problem
with your life apps. Let's explore how to fix them. By teaching you

how this software functions and how to make it run better, I'll show you the next step in mastering your expectations so you can begin to set them.

EXPECTATIONS 2.0

When it comes to our personal computing needs, hardware companies hire the best programmers in the world to write the latest operating system to keep our devices functioning properly. And then they continually improve it, based on new concepts and technology, so it will function as well as it possibly can. Imagine how crazy it would be if they were allowing their software to be written by novices who didn't understand what they were doing, why they were doing it, or what their output would be.

Well, that's essentially what we've allowed to happen when it comes to ourselves. The result is as dire as it would be for a computer: "Without software, the hardware wouldn't function," writes Dr. Bourgeois, and the same is true for us: without the proper programs, we can't be at our best.

We all must rewrite the software that runs our personal hardware so that our lives function optimally. If we don't, we will never maximize our potential, our perspective will be skewed, and we will never be completely free.

When you're driving, what would happen if your view was obstructed? Or if you didn't have a clear view of the road? You would crash. Now apply that fact to your life: maybe one reason why you aren't going where you want to go is that you can't see—you don't have a true perspective on yourself, others, or your experiences.

As we've already discussed, this can manifest itself in many ways, such as assumptions that have no basis in reality or judgments that cause you to draw incorrect conclusions about yourself, others, and any given situation. Maintaining perspective is an often-overlooked key to a successful, fulfilled life. Once lost, it can be very difficult to regain, especially when we're just going along with what's expected of us, whether or not we feel the pressure to do so or are aware of it.

As Dr. Bourgeois noted, there are two types of software: *operating systems* and *application software*. The operating system is responsible for several critical functions:

1. Managing the hardware resources of the computer
2. Providing the user-interface components
3. Providing a platform on which software developers can write applications

Our personal operating systems could be described as the way we see ourselves and talk to ourselves internally, the way we organize our lives, the habits we adopt. If you've lost perspective, or it's become impaired, you will think worse of yourself and others than is actually warranted. This idea is explored in the article we discussed earlier, "Why Judging Others Is Bad for You." Khoddam writes: "That same language we use to describe other people, objects, movies outside of us is often the same harsh and unforgiving language we turn to judge ourselves. 'I hate myself.' 'Why am I such an idiot?' . . . We don't see things for what they are, we see things through the lens of our mind."

This "lens" is really another term for "operating system." And it's a reminder that you are probably being harder on yourself than you deserve, and not giving yourself enough credit for how capable you are and for the many wins you've had. This is because your expectations are currently unset, and if you haven't examined them, they may be unrealistic. You see yourself as falling short when in reality you're not (or you're not falling short as badly as you think you are). Instead of judging yourself based on an expectation of what you hoped would happen, what about accepting where you are and appreciating what *has* happened? This is the key to rewriting the operating system running your life, right now. You can begin upgrading your software by getting clearer on how you currently function. Ask yourself:

- Did I program the software controlling how I see the world?
- If I didn't program my software, who did? Was it my parents? My upbringing, environment, or culture? Something else?
- When something doesn't go as I expect, how do I talk to myself internally about it?

Here's the takeaway: your software can be rewritten. As you gain control of your expectations and reprogram your life, you actually have the ability to rebuild how you think and behave in more positive and productive ways.

R.I.P., MR. PERFECT

I was running detrimental software for years before I began doing the work to reprogram myself. As we've already established, most of us have our software (meaning, our expectations) programmed for us in childhood, and we usually don't understand how we've been coded or see the repercussions of this coding in our adult lives.

I am the middle child of three boys. Growing up in Oakland, California, I was always fighting for my place in my family. (To all of the middle children reading this, I feel your pain!) There was a certain amount of chaos because my dad, Donald, was an alcoholic, which contributed to his premature death from a heart attack at age thirty-six. Until he died, he was in and out of the house, where I lived with my two brothers, Ray and Brandon, and my mom, Paulette. Although my parents never divorced, they were estranged, and my dad's presence was inconsistent. When he was alive, he had a habit of making promises to come spend time with my brothers and me that he wouldn't honor, without explaining why. I was too young to understand anything except my disappointment. I hated how that felt—like everything in my life was out of my control.

As I entered middle school, my craving for control and attention caused me to be very disciplined and focused, which led me to excel in the classroom and in leadership. The more I achieved, the more positive reinforcement I received, and my software was modified accordingly. From this I concluded: *In order to get attention, I need to achieve. And I can control this achievement.*

The problem was that this approach had an inverse logic as well, which gave rise to this dark, gnawing thought: *If I don't achieve this or that, then I'm not going to belong. I'm not going to be accepted.* What began to happen, over time, was that I put these very high standards on myself and was unrelenting in pursuing them, in the belief that the cost of not doing so would be devastating. (You ever been there before?) This right here is an example of an operating system of which I was completely unaware.

It was no accident that my nickname growing up was "Mr. Perfect." The scared part of me that needed validation took it as more fuel for the fire. I internalized the pressure of that ideal. Now, I *couldn't* make a mistake. I would think to myself, *If I make a mistake, then I'll no longer be perfect. And who will I be then?*

Think of that—my belief was that even the smallest mistake would have the direst consequences. Although it was all in my mind, the outcome I foresaw was terrifying enough to keep me from ever adjusting my standards. This belief informed so much of my approach to life; from adolescence through adulthood, my complete intolerance for mistakes meant I couldn't let up for a minute.

Being so driven led me to set many goals, and to achieve them. But even though I had the power to rewrite my own software, I lacked perspective. Instead, I was using my willpower to drive myself forward through my days. I had something to prove to myself, about my own self-worth, and I wasn't going to rest until I'd done so.

Looking back, I can see that there were many glitches in my software, but most people never would have known it. Internally, I experienced a great deal of frustration when things didn't happen as I wanted (or as quickly as I expected). I had a lot of anxiety and often demanded more of myself than was possible or realistic. Even when my perfectionism played out in negative ways (in self-judgment, or self-loathing), I was able to justify it by my demand for excellence in all areas. I mean, who's going to say there's anything wrong with wanting to be the best?

Well, as any of us who live this way will eventually discover, whenever we're hanging our value on outside achievements, we're heading for a fall. For a long time, total control was a big goal for me. Trying to *will* things to happen—that was my style. I engaged in negative self-talk on a daily basis, even when I seemed to be thriving. I achieved a great deal, but it never felt good enough, or like I was enough. It was not a healthy way for me to live. I'd based my expectations on my need to be perfect, which of course was unrealistic. And so I struggled for a long time with the fact that my expectations were unset and couldn't be set.

Darcy Cosper, a self-confessed perfectionist and overachiever, explored the ways in which perfectionists set themselves up for defeat, even if they're outwardly successful. Through her research, which included Dr. Allan E. Mallinger's book *Too Perfect: When Being in Control Gets Out of Control*, she found that many perfectionists develop this coping mechanism in response to childhood trauma (like me). As Cosper writes in her article for *Women's Health* magazine: "This unconscious belief persists into adulthood and can show up in a variety of ways, from obsessions with orderliness to workaholism. In the mind of the perfectionist, the need to get things just right becomes a way of ensuring personal survival."

Yes, exactly. Even years after I had created a great, stable life for myself as an adult, my old childhood fears still had way more power over my behavior than I realized. As I'll discuss when we examine professional expectations, it took driving myself nearly to a breaking point to eventually reject these toxic ways of thinking and operating.

Another revelation from Cosper was very familiar to me: many perfectionists spiral from setting lofty goals, which are a positive in and of themselves, into approaching them with rigidness and self-criticism for not ever doing or achieving enough.

The methods Cosper discovered for countering perfectionism are simple. They're also a good reminder that reprogramming is a constant process. Here are the steps she recommends for getting started on setting healthier personal standards: "I prioritize. . . . I try not to nitpick and obsess over unimportant details. I remind myself that 'perfect' isn't possible and strive to accept that the best I can do in the time that's available to me will have to be good enough."

While I've made great strides in this area, through careful self-reflection, prayer, and therapy, I'm still working on it. If you've struggled with perfectionism, as I have, I can guarantee that giving yourself a break will not only make you happier but also more effective. By prioritizing, while also being flexible about new opportunities and relationships that arise, your life will open up.

Now it's your turn. If your faulty software has skewed your perspective, ask yourself:

- Am I judging myself, or a person or experience in my life, based on unrealistic expectations?
- How can I align my expectations with reality and reprogram my personal software?

GET THE BUGS OUT OF YOUR OPERATING SYSTEM

Faulty operating systems have many different types of bugs. Mine was perfectionism. But a more common one is suppression, which can lead to self-destructive behaviors. This occurs when a trauma or feeling is buried. It may seem like your software is running fine, but it's actually been warped by your hidden pain, and it's causing you to act out in ways you can't see. Even if you can see the damage your behavior is causing to you and others, you feel like you are powerless to change it, to get your behavior under control. Until you release it, whatever you suppress is going to distort your software in unhealthy ways, whether it's overeating or overachieving. Anything done compulsively to avoid your feelings can be damaging.

Consider the Los Angeles–based DJ and radio personality Big Boy, who at one point weighed 510 pounds. He'd even made his size a part of his larger-than-life fame, which he'd achieved thanks to his quick wit and ease around the hottest hip-hop and Hollywood stars. Coming up, his size was actually an advantage when he worked as a bodyguard for The Pharcyde. He'd already become a popular LA party DJ, and now that he was known in the rap world, he parlayed his sense of humor into a job as a radio host for the LA hip-hop station Power 106. He cemented his legend with a series of popular billboards in the early 2000s that spoofed a then-ubiquitous Calvin Klein perfume ad by picturing a nearly naked 500-pound Big.

His life was changed by Will Smith in 2002. Will was one of the only people to call out Big on how unhealthy his weight was. He challenged Big, promising to donate $1,000 to charity for every pound Big lost, up to fifty pounds. Big launched a public weight loss campaign and shed an astonishing one hundred pounds. But without any work on his underlying issues, he soon gained it back.

In order to have the duodenal switch surgery that would eventually save his life, he was required to undergo therapy, but since his celebrity status led him to be fast-tracked through the process, it didn't help. The surgery was a success, in that it allowed him to keep off his excess weight, but he still had internal work to do on himself. For years he stayed in denial that there was any deeper issue behind his compulsive behaviors around food.

Finally, through the process of writing his memoir, *An XL Life: Staying Big at Half the Size*, Big underwent a personal reckoning. He admitted to his own root programming issue—emotional eating. He'd had a nomadic childhood, during which his single mom moved her six kids between motels in South Central Los Angeles. Unfortunately, because his mother often had no kitchen and was low on funds, she fed Big high-fat, high-sugar comfort food. He came to associate these dishes with her pure love, and that programmed him to eat too much of the wrong foods later in life.

When Big began recoding his own software, he called out many within the Black and Latino communities, urging them to rethink their expectations around health. But Big's message is universal. His goal is to spotlight what has been suppressed, and the true cost of suppressing it. He writes, "I think that, in order to be healthy, all of us need to start looking at our habits, especially the bad ones and where they came from."

ANYTHING WE SUPPRESS, WE EMPOWER.

Suppression is the equivalent of needing to clean up the house in a hurry, so you take all the clutter and throw it in the closet. Eventually, that closet is going to burst open unless you go in there and empty it out—through therapy, with the support of a pastor or life coach, or with the help of books like this one, designed to give you tools for nurturing your emotional well-being by shedding old beliefs and hurts that aren't serving you. When you have a feeling of pain from a childhood trauma, or losing your job, or having your heart broken, instead of reaching for the ice cream or the wine or the credit card, or whatever your vice may be, ride out the feeling. You can learn a new way to live. I'll explain how to do that in the pages that follow, where I'll teach you better tools for thinking about your life, communicating with others, and processing everything that happens to you. This upgrade will help you reprogram your software to thrive, even during the most difficult times.

WE ARE HOW WE THINK

Now that you know what needs to be done and why, it's time to begin the work on your own personal reboot. The first step is to embrace the immense possibility and flexibility of your mind and spirit, both of which have the capacity for tremendous transformation. Perspective allows you to see that even difficult times can contain gifts. A helpful guidebook for turning past loss into growth is Elizabeth Lesser's *New York Times* bestseller *Broken Open: How Difficult Times Can Help Us Grow*. She gathered lessons from inspiring stories of overcoming trauma in order to help people approach any challenge as the springboard for new opportunities and perspective.

One powerful passage on expectations draws inspiration from the legendary Auschwitz survivor and moral philosopher Victor Frankl, who said, "The last of the human freedoms [is] the freedom to choose one's attitude in any given set of circumstances." Frankl is essentially saying that we are free because we control how we think and feel about our past and about our current circumstances. While Lesser brings a great deal of compassion to her advice, she also bluntly tells readers that we are responsible for managing our own perspective, especially during difficult times: "If Victor Frankl was able to transform the despair of the death camps into a search for meaning, then we can do this too, even in our darkest moments. . . . Frankl discovered that 'it did not really matter what we expected from life, but rather what life expected from us.' "

Whether we're experiencing the most challenging trials imaginable or simply having an annoying day, we control our perspective, our response, and, ultimately, what we make of the hardship, whether for bad or, hopefully, for good, in terms of how we allow it to act on us.

Here's a word of advice, though. Sometimes you might need to reprogram your software repeatedly in order for the changes to really stick. Just think about how often you have to update your smartphone to keep it running at maximum efficiency. That's how operating systems work, and our mind is no exception.

It's all about follow-through, according to HR consultant and personal trainer George J. Ziogas in his piece "How to Reprogram Your Subconscious Mind: A Step by Step Guide": "Don't expect to see immediate changes. . . . Be very consistent and persistent with the methods you choose to install more positive messages into your subconscious mind. . . . Stick with it and know that these changes are lifelong, powerful and well worth waiting for!"

THE CHOICE IS YOURS

In the most powerful instances, this work to positively code your software will be transformative not only for you but also for those around you—maybe even those who helped write that original software in the first place. Take Nashville-based singer-songwriter Katie Pruitt. She grew up in a middle-class Catholic family in Georgia and attended weekly confession. Katie learned about sin and was taught that being gay, which she knew she was from a young age, was wrong. This created a painful secret that she was intent on keeping from her family and community.

When Katie began playing guitar and writing songs, she hid her real feelings in her lyrics. Finally, when she moved to Nashville, she had the courage to write "Loving Her," which celebrates her love for another woman and proudly defies those who might call it wrong. Such creative and personal freedom felt incredible, she said, especially when her new compositions led to a record deal with the folk label Rounder Records. Here was positive reinforcement that went against her programming—she could be herself and be accepted.

However, she still feared how her parents would receive her debut album, which she fittingly called *Expectations*. Still, she trusted that expressing her true self, even if it went against what was expected of her, was her only possible path in life.

In a National Public Radio interview about the album, Katie's mom, Jennifer, said it wasn't easy to listen to these songs—she had to come to terms not only with her daughter's sexuality but also with her pain, partly because of Jennifer's beliefs, and her fear of being rejected by her family.

Even though she had a strong desire to know and love her daughter's true self, Jennifer's path to acceptance took work: she read books, attended a faith-based support group, and listened hard to her daughter—both in her songs and in their sometimes painful conversations. It wasn't easy for Jennifer to shift her expectations about the right way to live, but for her the alternative was unacceptable: "I just had to go through what I had to go through to get to this place. And you know, that's what you do when you love somebody. That's what you do. It was like, okay, I'm not willing to not be part of my daughter's life over this."

Even with the great courage and compassion shown by both mother and daughter, overthrowing their previous expectations and reprogramming their software was a difficult and uncomfortable—painfully uncomfortable—process that didn't happen overnight. And yet, it did happen. Consider for a moment how much richer and more joyous both women's lives are now for having been able to grow and learn together and share their true selves.

That's what I want for all of you. That's why we're doing this work. It's actually possible to reprogram your software, and the benefits are life-changing, bringing freedom not only for you but for those you love too.

CHAPTER 2 Expectation Examinations

1. What are five beliefs you have about yourself, created by your secret software, that you know actually aren't true? What are five truer, more positive assessments of yourself?

2. Are there ways in which you're acting out because you're suppressing feelings about unrealistic expectations—either those you have of yourself or others' expectations of you?

3. Are you putting too much pressure on those around you?

4. What are five areas where you could move away from the obvious expectations around success or accomplishment and take a more profound and rewarding path?

5. When were five times you felt disappointed because your expectations, you now realize, were off? If your expectations had been more realistic, could those hurts have been avoided?

6. When were five times you hoped people in your life would do something that they never did? What has stopped you from forgiving them? Can you do so now?

3

SET YOURSELF UP FOR SUCCESS

I have learned that as long as I hold fast to my beliefs and values—and follow my own moral compass—then the only expectations I need to live up to are my own.

—MICHELLE OBAMA

False expectations take away joy.

—SANDRA BULLOCK

Unset expectations are a massive liability for you. They can create pressure, dissatisfaction, and unhappiness in your life, sometimes without you even being aware of what's at the root of these problems.

Now that you understand the basics of how expectations function, and why they can be dangerous, it's time to learn the power of setting your expectations in order to create success in all areas of your life.

SETTING EXPECTATIONS IS THE
PROCESS OF PROPERLY CHOOSING AND
COMMUNICATING EXPECTATIONS.

Think of setting expectations in the same way a doctor sets a broken bone. An unset broken bone is painful, debilitating, and likely to cause long-term damage if not treated correctly. Set properly, the fracture will heal in six to eight weeks, and in most cases the bone will be as strong as ever. I'll teach you how to be your own doctor, setting your expectations properly so that you will be stronger and not in pain.

The first step is to release as many expectations as possible. Let go of those you don't need by identifying which should stay and which should go. Resist the temptation to keep any expectation that isn't of your choosing. (This differs a bit when setting professional expectations, which I'll be covering in the last section.) You may not have chosen it because it is not really true to who you are and how you want to live, or because you realize that you have other priorities and goals that you've never acknowledged before.

When it comes to determining which expectations you should release and which you can keep and set, the rule is simple: **You should choose only those expectations that bring you joy.** Release any expectations that cause you pain or discomfort.

Joy is easy to define and feel. Look at any and all areas of your life and ask yourself:

- Does this expectation bring me joy?
- If this does not bring me joy, can I fix it, or should I release it?

Now, I know this is easier said than done, as so many of our expectations are actually based on what others (family, friends, and so on) expect of us. Truth be told, you may feel obligated to do what's expected of you, even if it's not in your heart, because you don't want to disappoint someone you care about. I understand—this is a hard position. But you have a decision to make:

ARE YOU GOING TO LIVE THE LIFE YOU EXPECT TO LIVE OR THE LIFE THAT'S EXPECTED OF YOU?

In order to live free, you must come out from underneath this burden of obligation. Consistently doing things you don't want to do can become a way of life (it may have already become the norm for you). The problem is that you end up paying for this choice. You bear the pain. But you do not have to live this way. You can change. However, it's going to require courage to release yourself from the burden of meeting any personal expectation that doesn't serve you.

Here are some additional questions you can ask yourself to help determine which of your expectations should be released or set:

- What or who in my life makes me feel uncomfortable because they're not compatible with my beliefs, values, or the person I want to be and/or the life I want to live?
- What makes me resentful because I feel like someone has pushed me into doing it?
- What causes me stress or wakes me up with a feeling of dread in the morning?
- What makes me feel bad about myself?

Move toward the expectations that feel good and resonate with your spirit (even if they are admittedly tough to meet) and away from those that don't.

WHAT'S IN IT FOR YOU?

Even something positive—like being a high achiever, for me—can become a negative if it's done for the wrong reasons. And making positive choices can also be a drain on you if you're not the one who's prioritizing them. This point was a convincing part of Joanna Holsten's argument for claiming greater personal freedom in her essay "Stepping Out of the Should Trap." Joanna takes readers through her own process of enlightenment about the damaging ways in which she had been thinking and living:

> "You should volunteer in the community" or "You should eat fruits and vegetables." While these may be evaluated as healthy behaviors, if they are coming from a place of obligation and external expectation, they are still doing damage. It wasn't until I figured out that the problem was both in the messages and the method that I was able to liberate myself from the "should" trap and live a more authentic life.

As Joanna points out, the "should trap" includes compromises and capitulations to the things you're expected to do but don't choose for yourself. They interfere with your ability to live a freer life. That's why you need to take so much care when you're setting your expectations and become a vigilant defender of your time and energy.

This is such an important step in setting your expectations. You must be brutally honest about anything you feel like you *have* to do but really don't want to do. You might be surprised at how much of your current life is filled with activities that fall into this category.

As discussed, a sense of obligation is one of the main things that imprisons us and keeps us from living free. We don't want to disappoint those close to us or ruin someone's image of who they think we are, so we commit to living by their set of expectations, not our own. This way of life is a joy killer! If we're being honest, you probably have too many obligations—so many that you have no time or energy for yourself. I'm not saying obligations are bad; we all have them. Yet, when we don't pause to evaluate and reassess how we are living and what is controlling our actions, we wind up living a life far different than the one we were created to live.

Stop and think about anything you're currently doing in your life that you really wish you weren't. What are you getting out of it *right now*?

Going forward, I want you to understand why you're doing what you're doing, and I want you to be clear on the benefits. You have to take full responsibility for your own joy.

**THE KEY TO YOUR HAPPINESS IS TO CAREFULLY
SET ALL OF YOUR EXPECTATIONS FOR YOURSELF.**

In *all* areas of your life, I want you to be crystal clear about your motivations. Stop doing things solely out of a feeling of obligation that comes from someone else's expectation. These are the questions I want you to get in the habit of asking yourself:

- What am I getting out of this conversation?
- What am I getting out of this friendship?
- What am I getting out of this job?
- What am I getting out of this church?
- What am I getting out of this relationship?

I have seen this concept make some people very uncomfortable. They protest: "Well, it's not about me. It's about putting others first." Yes, I'm all for putting others first—when we put ourselves first. The Bible says, "Love your neighbor as yourself." The emphasis is so often put on the neighbor part, but not on the self part. Maybe one of the reasons we don't love our neighbor well is because we aren't loving our own selves all that well. Another way to look at this idea is to say, "Take care of your neighbor's well-being in the same way you take care of your own well-being." This is why, when it comes to your joy, I'm not asking you to be selfish or self-centered—I'm asking you to prioritize yourself. Your life will go to another level when you learn this practice. Otherwise, you may begin to resent the people and obligations in your life, and you may never live free.

If you're feeling burdened by the sheer number of obligations in your life, it's hard to help somebody else to rise up. Self-prioritization helps you feel better because you're thinking through your needs, your life, and your joy. Filled cups fill cups. **If you feel better, you're going to do better.** When you're more joyful, you can be of even better service to others.

Plus, it will be so much easier to maintain a healthy perspective. If you're sacrificing for a goal, or a person, you'll do so with greater purpose and a lighter heart. You'll be saying: *You know what? I'm making this sacrifice, because it also meets my needs.*

Ask yourself:

- What's something on my calendar that I'm doing only because I feel like I should?
- Who decided that I "should" do this thing, and do I care if I disappoint them?
- What's the worst thing that can happen if I say no to this obligation?
- Is there another way I could spend this time that would be more meaningful for me?
- If I absolutely must fulfill this necessary obligation—maybe it's a parent-teacher conference, or a dentist appointment—is there a way I can change my perspective to be more positive?

I guarantee that self-prioritizing and letting go of even a few obligations that have felt like a drain on your time and energy will make you feel so much happier right away. And when you start filling that free time with more meaningful activities, you'll feel even more fulfilled. Remember, though, that "should" is a two-way street. If someone in your life does not want to do something that you feel like they "should," it's up to you to respect their boundaries, just as you'd want them to do for you. They have as much right to set their own expectations as you do.

YOU BE YOU FOR YOU, NOT FOR THEM

Although it's simple, setting expectations is not always a conflict-free undertaking. As we've established, part of the process is internal; however, a critical part of the process is external. It involves communicating your expectations, starting with yourself, and then communicating with others in your life. Sometimes when others are involved when you're trying to set expectations, there will be pushback. However, don't let that stop you from setting your expectations.

Since so many of our expectations come from our loved ones, a major obstacle to setting them for ourselves might be the fear of disappointing or upsetting the very people we love and care for so much.

In my experience, this is one of the main obstacles you will face when doing this work. For years you've made a habit of making your loved ones happy, often at the expense of your own happiness. So their response when you start to communicate that the way you've been living is no longer okay, or that you aren't going to do something any longer, simply because you're expected to do it, may create tremendous conflict. They may not know how to process the shift in you, if you don't do what you've always done, in the same way they've always expected you to do it.

Sometimes the people closest to you may even try to stop you from setting your expectations for yourself, especially if they're not in line with those they believe you *should* be setting for yourself. Although other people's feelings are involved, that doesn't mean you should fake it, or sell yourself out, all in the name of someone else's happiness. Not if you're going to live free.

Here's a perfect example, involving a writer, producer, and actress I greatly admire, Issa Rae. Even though she created and stars in the hit HBO comedy *Insecure*, she has had to fight to set her own expectations. Her father, a self-made doctor who had very strong opinions about his daughter going to medical school, sent Issa to a specialized high school where aspiring doctors got a head start by volunteering in hospitals. The experience was valuable for her, as she told the *Atlantic*, but not in the way her dad had expected or hoped: it made her realize that she definitely didn't want to be a doctor. Her dad responded to this revelation by suggesting law or business school. She wavered, and then she had an epiphany: "My second year of college, when I was pursuing political science, and I had to declare the major and answer the question 'Why do you want to pursue political science?,' all I could think of was *Because my dad wants me to*. That was a wake-up call: He's not living my life, I am!"

Yes, that is absolutely right. And if Issa Rae had given in to her dad and actually gone through with all of that medical schooling and a residency, not only would she have been miserable, but the world would have missed out on her unique talents.

Do you see what's at stake if you keep living to meet the expectations of other people about your life instead of your own? Issa had to choose her own way, even though her dad didn't agree with her choices. While it was difficult, in the end the benefit was positive— for her and for all of us.

Here are some more questions for you to explore. Ask yourself:

- Are there any expectations I would give up if it wouldn't disappoint my loved ones?
- Do I know for a fact that my loved ones wouldn't accept my decision?
- Have I experienced pain because of my loved ones' reactions to my choices? If yes, what am I doing to heal the pain?

GET OUT (OF THE BOX)

Once again, I'm not telling you anything that I haven't already put into practice myself—with immediate and powerful results. Even though I'm a producer and an author, I've always preached on the side. In the past, it was my habit to say yes to pretty much every invitation I received to preach. By early 2020, I was being asked to preach more and more. At first, I kept saying yes to everything. That was what I had always done, and it felt good to be of service. But after a few months, I realized I needed to examine how preaching fit into my life and my overall impact in the world. I was really honest with myself and asked: *Wait a minute. Why am I doing this? Why am I preaching so much?*

I had started preaching at fifteen years old, when I was asked to speak at our church's second annual Youth Day. My older brother had spoken at the first one. Since I was outgoing and very involved in our church, I wasn't surprised when my aunt Sondra, who was head of our youth ministry, asked me to preach. In addition to the Bible, I studied Les Brown's book *Live Your Dreams* to prepare for my sermon. I spoke on the topic of staying focused. On that day, I was nervous and excited, but I stepped into the pulpit and did my best. To my surprise, it went even better than I could have imagined. People in the pews were shouting "Amen" and "Hallelujah." After it was over, so many people came up to me and said, "Oh, you were amazing. You've got to become a preacher." From that day, even after establishing my primary career in Hollywood, I've always preached in some capacity. It's not that I ever wanted to stop preaching completely, but simply that I'd started to become lost and confused about my identity.

I knew that I was no less committed to my faith. The problem was that I was starting to feel like I was putting myself in a box—the preacher box—and then putting all of these expectations on myself that go along with that role. Like, if I was going to preach so much, then I should be working toward having my own church, but I knew in my heart that wasn't what God was calling me to do. When I got real with myself, I acknowledged that these were not goals I was moving toward. When I looked at my overall impact, I saw that other aspects of my gifts—like producing, writing, and motivating—were giving me unique ways to reach people that went beyond what I could do in any pulpit. This does not mean that I don't love and value preaching. What it does mean is that preaching is just one of the things I do; it's not who I am. It means that I set the expectations for when, where, and how often I will preach. No one else but me (and God of course).

Again, this wasn't a question of juggling items on my calendar; this was about my need to live my true identity, one that couldn't be defined by a label. What I realized was that I'd been feeling like I was in this box for so long that I had lost myself—my true self, my unique self, with my own special purpose. That was why I had been feeling so uneasy.

As soon as I achieved clarity on this, I realized that no one was putting me in this box except for me. And that if I didn't want these expectations to be put on me, then I had to be the one to climb out of the box. Even though I knew it was right for me to step back from preaching so much, I still had a moment of hesitation. I wondered, *What will this mean for me? Will I upset people? Will I lose my place in this world?*

Don't be afraid of being afraid. Yes, it's scary to change everything you think you know about yourself. Move forward anyway. As my mentor says, "The life you want is on the other side of whatever you fear." I pushed ahead—only to be met with the resistance I had dreaded. When I told my team that I'd had a clear message from God that I should preach less, they pushed back on me. "No, you've got to keep preaching. People are expecting you to keep preaching."

And so I kept doing it, because it was *expected*. Mind you, I'm the expert over here, writing the book on setting expectations, but it was hard even for me to say no. Finally, after a few months, I couldn't deny the truth. As much as I love preaching, I was losing my joy in it. So I approached my team again: "Listen, people are going to live if I stop preaching, right? I've got to be obedient to what I feel, and I can't live up to their expectations anymore. I'm not saying I'm never going to preach again. Of course, I'll preach again. But I have to pull back right now. People may be angry, and they may be hurt, but their disappointment, God can handle."

I stood my ground. I took on fewer preaching engagements, and do you know what was on the other side of that decision? Joy. Freedom. More space to think, to live, and to be who I really am, to figure out what's really important to me and to start doing even more of that. Easing up on my preaching schedule has allowed me more time for self-reflection and self-revelation. *Who am I? What do I really want to do? How do I want to use this gift? What is my impact in the world?*

Answering these questions also helped me let go of a few other obligations that weren't really in my heart to do. And then, from this place of greater self-knowledge and self-acceptance, I began setting my expectations all over again. It's a lifetime process, and one that you improve at with practice, to the point where it finally becomes automatic.

Sometimes it's easier to be busy, to throw yourself into something, so you don't have to think for yourself. You're on autopilot. You might even be experiencing a little bit of avoidance, unwilling to face what you really need to do. It's harder to be alone with ourselves, finding our true path, setting our expectations, than it is to do what's right in front of us. It can be easier to go along with the expectations of others, even if it's uncomfortable, than to face the challenge of stopping and building our own lives, based on our true calling. But we must stop in order to do so.

Since I set my expectations in this new way, preaching has felt like an expression of the gift that it is, not something I do because I should. I'm so much happier and freer, and I believe my message is clearer and stronger. I'm walking the walk I'm preaching about. As I've told others to do, I've found my purpose, and I'm staying true to it. I'm setting my own expectations, and I'm living up to them on my terms. I'm living free.

Now it's your turn. Ask yourself:

- What are three things I'm doing right now that are taking up most of my energy?
- What do I really want to do?
- How do I want to use my gift?
- What is my impact in the world, and is it what I really want it to be?

On the other side of answers to these questions is your free self and your free life—and your joy.

CHAPTER 3 Expectation Examinations

1. Take the list of personal expectations you made back in chapter 1 and do a "Joy v. Pain" assessment. Next to each expectation that brings you joy put a **J**, and next to the expectations that bring you pain put a **P**.

2. How many expectations that you marked with a **P** can you release right now?

3. If you can't release an expectation, why not? If you know it's something that's important to another person, can you shift your POV so it's no longer their expectation of you but your gift to them?

4. If an expectation came from your parents, can you simply release it? Or are you feeling lingering resentment or pain about their expectation that you need to discuss with them before you can heal yourself and fully release the expectation?

5. If you fear that releasing an expectation held by your family is going to cause them to be angry or even reject you, what support do you have in place to weather a transition to a place of being free to be yourself? Do you have a therapist, pastor, or trusted friend you can keep on speed dial?

4

YOUR EXPECTATIONS ARE UNREALISTIC

The number-one reason for ethical violations is the pressure to meet expectations—sometimes unrealistic expectations.
—STEPHEN COVEY

I would like my car to fly and make me breakfast, but that's an unrealistic expectation.
—JACK TRETTON

You're in an expectation crisis, and you might not even realize it. This is understandable, given that you're being bombarded with unrealistic expectations on all fronts, all of the time, and so it's easy to take them on for yourself.

WE LIVE IN AN AGE OF
UNREALISTIC EXPECTATIONS.

Look at advertising—billions of dollars are earned annually from feeding us the myth that a product or outfit can instantly turn us into the best version of ourselves. When you break it down, an ad or a commercial is essentially an unattainable aspiration in disguise. They are *everywhere*—at the gas pump when we fill our tank, in the back seats of taxi cabs, and in the media we consume. The negative impact is immediate and profound.

In a three-decade study reported in the *Harvard Business Review*, more than 900,000 citizens of twenty-seven European countries were surveyed and asked the straightforward question: "How satisfied are you with your life?" The study concluded that for every dollar spent in a country on advertising in a year, there was a corresponding decline in the happiness of its residents.

When advertising spending doubled, there was a 3 percent drop in satisfaction, according to researcher Andrew Oswald of the University of Warwick, who was on the team that conducted the study. He described this decrease as equivalent to "about half the drop in life satisfaction you'd see in a person who had gotten divorced or about one-third the drop you'd see in someone who'd become unemployed. We have a lot of experience working out how people are affected by bad life events, and advertising has sizable consequences even when compared with them."

As Oswald broke it down, advertising really does create unrealistic expectations within us, by causing us to compare ourselves to others and making us feel less satisfied with our possessions—and by extension, with our lives and with ourselves:

We know from lots of research that making social comparisons can be harmful to us emotionally, and advertising prompts us to measure ourselves against others. If I see an ad for a fancy new car, it makes me think about my ordinary one, which might make me feel bad. . . . I might think, "Maybe there's something wrong with me."

On top of advertising, there's TikTok, Instagram, Facebook, YouTube, Twitter, Twitch, and so on—social media is full of unrealistic expectations about how we should look and live. Most of us feel some form of this pressure on a daily basis, and sometimes it leads to depression and anxiety. We're not alone. In 2018, the BBC reported that social media caused more than half of the 1,500 people surveyed by the disability charity Scope to feel "inadequate," and half of them, between the ages of eighteen and thirty-four, to feel "unattractive."

You see what other people are doing—or represent as what they're doing, whether it's true or not—and then it's very easy to begin to compare yourself to them, consciously or subconsciously, or to want something you otherwise would never want.

Not to mention the number of negative comments that are posted on social media, full of judgment and criticism. If you're the target, that can make you feel even worse about yourself. You might even become upset if you post something and it doesn't earn as many likes as you wanted. The real problem happens when you put all of this pressure on yourself because of what you see other people doing, achieving, and possessing. It all adds up to a major drain on your system.

WHAT IS AN UNREALISTIC EXPECTATION?

I hate to burst your bubble, but most of your expectations are probably unrealistic. This is why you are so frustrated. You are trying to achieve something that isn't based in reality. Now, before you call me a pessimist, hear me out. I am an admitted faith addict! I love faith and live by it every day. But I work on living by faith while taking in the full reality of my world, good and bad—a critical process that has helped me to set realistic expectations. I've learned the hard way that the more we try to control what's out of our control, the more frustrated and deeply dissatisfied we will remain with life. This is why I need you to understand what realistic expectations really mean and how they function.

The difference between unrealistic and realistic expectations comes down to one word: *control*. When the results you want are within your power to make happen, then your expectations are realistic. But anytime you expect anything that's outside of your control, your expectations are unrealistic.

> **WHATEVER IS IN YOUR CONTROL**
> **IS REALISTIC TO EXPECT.**

Whatever isn't in your control is dangerous, and unrealistic to expect.

While this is a simple concept, the major obstacle we often face when it comes to setting realistic expectations is our denial of it. Admitting that we are powerless over most aspects of our lives—and especially the areas we really care about—can be challenging.

UNREALISTIC EXPECTATIONS
ARE FUTURE RESENTMENTS

One of the areas where unrealistic expectations can do the most damage is in our relationships with other people. Plain and simple, they are the seed for future resentments. In an article for *Psychology Today*, "The Psychology of Expectations," John A. Johnson, PhD, breaks it down like this: "The problem of expectation occurs when we expect something to happen without good reasons for that expectation. . . . Expectations are premeditated resentments."

When we are analyzing our expectations that involve other people to determine if they are realistic or not, we must always remember that we don't control anyone—not our spouse, not our children, not our friends, not our family, not even our employees. We only control ourselves. We can ask other people to do something. We can create consequences if they don't comply with our request. But anything beyond that is skating toward the realm of unrealistic expectations and the resentments they breed.

Many of us get into exactly this type of trouble, though, because most relationships come with an "implicit social contract." Generally, there's nothing wrong with this. The problem occurs when we assume that our each and every desire will be met exactly as we want it to be, sometimes without even expressing our need to the other person. Obviously, this is not a failing on the other person's part; it's our own failure to properly set our expectations. Still, we continue to allow our emotions to entangle us.

Dr. Johnson provides a more realistic, and potentially positive way to look at your expectations instead: "Believing that an unverbalized expectation will bring you what you want is magical thinking and is unrealistic. . . . Expecting others to do what is in your interest, but not their interest, is unrealistic."

Unrealistic expectations distort your perspective. If they're not met in the way you want them to be, and in the time frame you've set, you can end up frustrated or completely depressed. If you don't meet the unrealistic expectations of others, you might turn to suppression and self-destructive behavior. Or you might rebel against what feels like unfair standards, even though doing so could jeopardize your relationships and your personal well-being. Whether you're trying to live up to unrealistic expectations, projecting them onto others, or having them projected onto you, they are hazardous. They blind you to your worth, your blessings, and the reality that even personal failures can be stepping-stones to greater triumphs.

Look at the main relationships in your life—family, work, romantic—and ask yourself:

- Is someone in my life projecting an unrealistic expectation onto me? (For example, maybe a friend wants you to call them as often as they call you.)
- Am I expecting something of someone else that is unrealistic? (For example, maybe you want your friend to always like and comment on your social media posts.)

Waiting for someone to do something that is not within their power to do is like waiting to win the lottery without buying a ticket. And yet, we've all been caught in cycles where we've done this when it comes to other people—and even ourselves.

THE PRESSURE TO LIVE UP TO WHAT ISN'T REAL

No one is immune. Even those people who seem, on the surface, to be excelling in their field and living as their best selves have admitted to struggling with feeling less than, because of the unrealistic expectations that were projected onto them by others.

Just take the world's most decorated female gymnast in history, Simone Biles, who won four Olympic gold medals, a record for the most gold medals earned by an American woman gymnast at a single Olympic games, plus a bronze medal, not to mention more than two dozen medals at the World Championships over the years. Plus, she's cowritten a *New York Times* bestselling memoir, *Courage to Soar: A Body in Motion, a Life in Balance,* which debuted at number one and was adapted into a Lifetime biopic. She's also earned sponsorships from the likes of Nike and United Airlines. In other words, Simone is an incredibly accomplished person. And yet, she has struggled with the negative impact that online trolls have had on her self-image, as she admitted during an interview on *Good Morning America* in March 2020: "In the beginning I would go look through comments, and I would cry, or maybe I would comment back to some. . . . I really started to study them. If they were like, 'Oh, your nose is too big,' I was like, 'Oh my gosh, you're right, it is too big.' "

With self-work, she has achieved greater perspective and no longer gives power to negative comments by people who don't know her beyond her looks and accomplishments. She's also committed herself to speaking out against unrealistic ideals related to appearance and the unkind ways in which they can be propagated online. She partnered with the skin-care line SK-II to launch #NOCOMPETITION, a campaign challenging current beauty standards and featuring other athletes who have felt the same pressures. At the time of its launch in February 2020, she posted a letter on Instagram about the negative impact of competition in her own life:

> Let's talk about competition. Specifically, the competition I didn't sign up for and feel like has become an almost daily challenge for me. And I do not think I am the only one. In gymnastics, as in many other professions, there is a growing competition that has nothing to do with performance itself. I'm talking about beauty. I don't know why, but others feel as though they can define your own beauty, based on their standards.

I applaud Simone for pushing back on unhealthy standards that have been elevated to societal norms. I also think the fact that there's a need for this campaign in the first place is a powerful indicator of how widespread—and damaging—this expectation crisis is. And beauty is only one area of many in which people are feeling unable to compete or keep up.

Most of us absorb these kinds of insidious, unrealistic expectations on a daily basis without even being aware of it. And when we don't identify them as such but try to set them as expectations for ourselves, we become caught in a cycle of striving and failing and, too often, blaming ourselves for not doing or being enough. If this discontent makes us think less of ourselves or feel burnt out, we blame ourselves, then often buy something to fix it. We need to examine that automatic and subconscious process so we can see that many of these expectations are unrealistic—and so we can climb off the wheel and start really living, by only setting those expectations that are both realistic and in line with our true values.

The first step is to identify a few of these pressures in your own life, so you can release them. Ask yourself:

- Who or what have I seen online or in an ad that made me buy or do something to compete?
- Did I achieve the response or feeling I'd hoped for, or did it actually make me feel worse?
- What's one thing about my body, life, or possessions that I could accept now exactly as it is?
- What's one unrealistic expectation I could release and replace with a realistic one?

THE COST OF STRIVING TOO HIGH (PARENTS, BE CAREFUL)

Even before the widespread layoffs and financial instability brought on by the Covid-19 pandemic, we were living in a hypercompetitive education and employment environment. Today concerned parents might feel like their kids—if they don't push them early—will fall behind in the future. But research shows that blind academic aspiration leads to unrealistic expectations, which actually have a high *negative* cost to the performance of students.

A five-year study of 3,500 secondary school students and their parents in Bavaria, Germany—which was replicated with 12,000 American students and their parents—made a clear distinction between the value of aspirations versus expectations: "While high parental aspirations led to increased academic achievement, that occurred only when parents' expectations were realistic, the researchers found. When their aspirations exceeded what their children could reasonably achieve, the adolescents' achievement declined, they found."

The researchers did not mince words when criticizing unrealistic expectations for their negative impact on kids, as reported in the American Psychological Association's *Journal of Personality and Social Psychology*. According to the study's lead author, Kou Murayama, PhD, of the University of Reading: "Our research revealed both positive and negative aspects of parents' aspiration for their children's academic performance. Although parental aspiration can help improve children's academic performance, excessive parental aspiration can be poisonous."

The researchers' report went on to say that programs aimed at helping parents increase their children's academic success would actually have better results if they focused on helping parents have more realistic expectations of what their children could achieve, rather than blindly urging them always to do better. This is such an important distinction. It wasn't a problem that the parents encouraged their children to excel; it only became a problem when parents' standards were higher than their kids could realistically achieve.

Again, this is why comparison can be so dangerous. Obviously, each student is going to have a different benchmark for what they can accomplish, and each parent will need to adjust their expectations for that child accordingly, rather than chasing a symbol of success equal to or greater than that of other families. It's up to every person to be responsible for setting their own expectations at a realistic level.

EXPECTATIONS FROM THE SCHOOL OF ROCK

You might be struggling at this very moment with unrealistic expectations. You're not alone. Just take Dwayne "The Rock" Johnson. In a 2019 motivational speech (which has been viewed nearly nine million times), he describes how certain he was that football was his ticket out of his troubled childhood, during which he had been arrested eight or nine times for fighting and theft before he was seventeen. As a college freshman, he played well as a defensive lineman for the Miami Hurricanes, and his prospects looked even better for his sophomore year. He was sure this was *it*—his direct path to the NFL and to living his dreams.

Unfortunately, even with all of his hard work, his unrealistic expectation that he would become a star athlete was not within his control. His teammate Warren Sapp, who was an even stronger defensive lineman, usurped his spot, and then injuries sidelined Johnson further. By his early twenties, he'd been cut from the Hurricanes and had failed to make the roster of any team in the Canadian Football League or any team in the NFL, whose draft he entered in 1995. Any hope of a pro football career was over. With his dreams dashed, he moved back in with his parents. Of course, many young people don't have a smooth transition into their adult life and need a little help from Mom and Dad. But because of how sure he'd been about where he was headed, Johnson was devastated: "This is not supposed to be in my future. I'm supposed to be in the NFL right now, making a lot of coin and taking care of my wife. But it never happened."

Remember when we talked about the dangerous ways in which expectations can become assumptions? This type of magical thinking is especially problematic when we start off with an unrealistic expectation without realizing it. Then we're automatically forming an assumption based on unsound data. The Rock's football dream was out of his control, no matter how hard he trained, and when that became clear to him, he was shattered.

Fortunately, he soon had the profound realization that this was the case, and it would shape his future: the problem hadn't been with his performance or his dedication, but with the fact that he'd been sidelined by matters out of his control. What he *could* influence was the effort he brought to everything he undertook going forward. Even though he was emotionally shattered by not making it as a professional football player, he didn't wallow for long or spiral into inactivity or depression from the frustration of that setback. He regrouped and exploded onto the scene as a professional wrestler for WWE, which eventually led to his most successful career—as one of the biggest movie stars in the world. Eventually, he used his disappointment to motivate himself. As he said in his speech: "When shit goes bad, and it goes sideways, a lot of shit does . . . you've got to keep it in here," he said, indicating his chest. "And it really has to, it should drive you."

The Rock is someone who's understandably a role model for so many, and yet, even he had moments when he was upset, in part, because of his own unrealistic expectations. But he was able to make a profound shift in his thinking and his life by focusing on realistic expectations—those things within his control, like his work ethic. Today, later in his life, he seems well aware that one of the only things he does control is the amount of effort he puts into anything he wants to bring to fruition. That is a great lesson for us all.

WHAT YOU ACTUALLY CAN CONTROL

We've spent a whole chapter talking about everything in your life that you can't control. Finally, here's a little good news. While you can't control the future outcome of most events (any more than you can control people), there is something even more important that *is* within your control: your present happiness. That's according to a new study, called "Tracking Happiness," which asked 1,154 participants questions about their perception of how happiness functions and about how happy they were in the previous year. Those who believed they could control their happiness were measurably happier than those who didn't, as summarized in the *Forbes* article by Bryan Robinson, PhD, "Can You Control Your Happiness? New Study Gives a Scientific Backed Answer." The numbers are clear: 89 percent of those surveyed said happiness could be controlled. Those who thought so had an overall happiness rating of 7.39 (on a 10-point scale), as opposed to the 5.61 happiness rating of those who didn't. As Robinson concluded:

> The happiest people learn over time how to implement strategies that give them an upper hand at being happy, which inoculates them against the curve balls that life throws their way. Focusing on the aspects of our lives that we can control versus focusing on what we can't control makes a big difference in our pursuit of happiness.

So, maintaining the expectation that we can control our happiness is one of those few, carefully chosen expectations that we do want to keep and cultivate. But here's a friendly reminder too: as soon as we put any qualifiers on when or why we'll be happy, we're right back to where we started, with potentially detrimental unrealistic expectations that we need to release. Don't say, "I'll be happy when I'm promoted next year." Don't even say: "I'll be happy when I'm promoted." Instead, say:

"I'll be happy right now, and any future happiness will happen because I've already been practicing happiness."

It's a subtle shift in your POV, but one that can have a profound and immediate impact on how you feel and how you experience your life.

You may still be wondering, *But how do I choose to be happy? Sure, that sounds good, in theory, but how do I actually practice happiness?* You choose to be happy by shifting your focus away from the results you seek and onto the process you cultivate every day. Since the results are often out of your control, putting your focus there won't lead to true happiness in the same way that learning to love the process will. (I'll go into the specifics of how to make this shift in the next section.) This shift can and should be applied to all areas of your existence. And I can tell you from firsthand experience that a shift in your perspective will create an immediate uptick in your feeling of overall satisfaction and happiness, and the positive outcomes will grow from there.

So, start by releasing any expectations related to things in your life that are controlled by other people, as well as all expectations that are unrealistic for any other obvious reasons. And then do it again, every day, forever. As I've said, this is a practice. But waiting patiently for you on the other side is what you actually can control: your happiness.

CHAPTER 4 Expectation Examinations

1. Pick an expectation you want to set. Ask yourself if it's actually realistic. If it's not, is there a way to make it more realistic, so that it can be set? If you need to release it, what other expectation could you set for yourself instead that is realistic?

2. List five areas where you know a physical expectation is unrealistic, but you still feel pressure to achieve it—such as whiter teeth, washboard abs, or an expensive outfit.

   i. Next to each of these five items, write down what it would
     take to flip your expectation from unrealistic to realistic. Is this
     something you can afford or are willing to do?

  ii. For any item you've deemed as unrealistic or unattainable, given
     your current circumstances, what will it take for you to release
     this expectation and be at peace with the reality of how you
     look, or with the best outcome you can possibly achieve?

3. List three moments in your past when you were let down because
something didn't happen as you wanted it to. Looking back, were your
expectations realistic?

4. List three moments in your past when someone in your life was
severely disappointed in you. Were their expectations realistic?
Looking back, could you have done something differently to better
bridge the gap between what they expected and what you were willing
or able to do?

5. What is your biggest source of interpersonal stress right now? It
could be stress between you and your spouse, your boss, a neighbor, a
sibling—anyone close to you. Be really honest: Do you have unrealistic
expectations about this person that are at the root of your frustration?
What would be a more realistic expectation of this person's behavior
or attitude?

5

YOUR EXPECTATIONS MUST BE COMMUNICATED

Great communication begins with connection.
—Oprah Winfrey

Compassionate people ask for what they need. . . . They're compassionate because their boundaries keep them out of resentment.
—Brené Brown

Many people struggle with communication. Scratch that. Almost *everyone* does. I think of myself as an effective communicator and even I, at times, have trouble communicating my expectations clearly. But it's a crucial tool for mastering your reality and moving toward a life of freedom.

Once you have determined that an expectation is realistic and of your choosing, you must express it to whoever else is involved (even to yourself if it's an expectation you have of yourself).

**EXPECTATIONS AND COMMUNICATION
GO HAND IN HAND.**

As long as your expectations remain unspoken, you won't succeed in setting them. So, let's look at the problems created by uncommunicated expectations. The first hurdle is that we often feel like we shouldn't have to explain why something is important to us or come right out and ask for it. We're so accustomed to our own perspective on life that we often forget that what is obvious to us may not be so obvious to those around us, even those who care deeply about our well-being. News flash: People aren't mind readers. It's up to us to communicate our needs. Now's the time to get clear on what you've been expecting from other people, and whether or not these expectations can be set.

To begin, ask yourself:

- Is there an expectation I'd like to set that I haven't communicated yet?
- Why haven't I spoken up? Am I afraid I won't get the answer or support I want?
- Can I reframe my expectation, so I'll be okay with whatever answer I get?

LEARN YOUR ABCs

The truth is that most of us are never taught how to communicate. So many parents bring their own family baggage into this area when raising the next generation. In his 2014 memoir *Manhood*, my friend the actor and comedian Terry Crews recounts several painful scenes from his childhood when his alcoholic father's inability and unwillingness to communicate with him created tension within the family and cracks in Terry's foundational confidence. After years of bearing the brunt of his father's mercurial and often unkind ways, and witnessing his frequent abuse of his mother, Terry had an epiphany as a teenager:

> My dad certainly wasn't teaching me anything. In fact, he was always telling me to do something he'd never explained to me before—like the time he made me change the oil in my mother's car—and then, when I did it wrong, he got mad at me. That hurt me badly. I didn't understand how he could expect me to know something I'd never been taught.

Unfortunately, many people grow up this way, essentially raising themselves and doing the best they can to learn what they need to know in life. For Terry, the pain from his childhood drove him to build up his physique and strength as a form of protection, while suppressing his feelings. That led to a secret pornography addiction, for which he eventually sought treatment.

At the same time, Terry, who had a longtime passion for self-help books, was always striving to learn and grow and better himself. And what he came to realize was that he'd been purposely withholding communication from his wife, as he told the dating website eharmony.com around the time his book was published. But after he saw the problems and lack of true intimacy created in his marriage by a lack of communication, he reprogrammed himself:

> I remember when I wouldn't tell my wife certain things, even about myself, in order to control her. It was an attempt, by lack of information, to give her a picture and an image

that wasn't really true . . . but the real deal is when someone knows all your thoughts, and knows everything that you've done wrong and knows all your problems, and they still love you, the relationship will go forever.

Although Terry gave this advice in the context of a romantic relationship, it has a valuable application here as well. His experience shows our capacity to grow in our lives, even if we started out with a deficit in an important area, such as communication. Terry went from being someone who hadn't been given any of the tools he needed in relationships to someone who developed himself into such an expert that a dating website asked him to give advice to its readers. You too have done the work in the previous chapters to overcome and release the deficits from your past, and now, in order to upgrade your existence across the board, you're almost ready to share your carefully chosen expectations with those closest to you.

Let's also look at one of the self-improvement classics, *How to Win Friends and Influence People*. This perennial bestseller, written by Dale Carnegie and published in 1936, has sold more than 15 million copies. In his first chapter, "If You Want to Gather Honey, Don't Kick Over the Beehive," Carnegie draws on many examples of great leaders and thinkers to establish the importance of your approach: "Benjamin Franklin, tactless in his youth, became so diplomatic, so adroit at handling people, that he was made American Ambassador to France. The secret of his success? 'I will speak ill of no man,' he said. '. . . and speak all the good I know of everybody.' "

You don't have to be a statesman or a business leader to benefit from better communication skills and greater tact. As you enter into conversation with your spouse, child, parent, best friend, or loved one do not lead with any anger you might be feeling. It will work against creating an environment of understanding and accord. The person you're communicating with didn't have the information they needed to understand what you were expecting. Now's your opportunity to clearly communicate your expectations to them.

IT'S NOT ALWAYS EASY TO HEAR NO

Here's one of the most challenging aspects about setting expectations: You can have a realistic expectation that involves another person. You can communicate it clearly, in an attempt to set it. But you have to accept that, even if you verbalize it, and request for it to be met, the other person is not obligated to agree to it. Also, if you don't like their decision to say no to your expectation, you are the one who has to work through your feelings instead of blaming them for being unwilling to meet whatever your expectation may have been.

On the other hand, you shouldn't skip something you're called to do if the other person isn't feeling it—just as you shouldn't expect them to give up something that's meaningful to them. And you shouldn't avoid a conversation, on any subject, simply because you don't want to hear no. Whatever the truth of the situation, it will be better for both parties to be fully informed and to accept it.

For any relationship or friendship to function well, both parties need to be allowed to say no to obligations and agreements if saying yes is not in their heart to do. But even when you make allowances for the other person's needs and boundaries, of course you're still going to have some feelings going down. That's okay. It doesn't mean it's a bad relationship. Quite the contrary—being able to build a dynamic that can hold the feelings of both people involved is quite an accomplishment, and not always an easy one. The key to doing that is communication.

For all of your significant relationships, regular conversation is necessary to make sure you're in accord about the priorities of the relationship, and that you and the other person are both having your needs met. An important factor to keep in mind is that people and their priorities change with time, and so there may need to be new negotiations around previously set expectations. The more comfortable you can become with this information exchange, and the less attached you are to getting the precise outcome you desire, the easier it will be for you to handle the fluid nature of most relationships.

That said, even after all the work around expectations I've already done, sometimes I still have to stop and ask myself: *Am I reacting to the reality of the situation, or am I reacting to my expectation of what I thought it* should *be?*

Similarly, if we disappoint the expectations of someone close to us, they will probably have feelings about it. We might have to make space for their feelings, while staying true to what we're called in our heart to do (or not do). And we also might have to watch ourselves, to make sure we don't project onto them by telling ourselves that their anger means that they don't care about us. No, their anger is their issue, not ours, and they might simply need time to readjust.

It's healthy to have feelings, but you do need to work through them, so you can release any negative ones. And if you could use some help and support to do so, it's okay to get it, whether from a therapist, life coach, or trusted friend. Untended negative feelings can fester and cause resentment, much like unexpressed expectations. Both can take root and become very detrimental and destructive to you.

If issues are coming up in this area, there may be a deeper issue at play. It could be time to ask yourself if you're putting too much on the other person—like expecting them to *make* you happy (I will go deeper into this dynamic in part 3, "Relational Expectations"). We know deep down this expectation isn't fair, or right, or sustainable, but sometimes we're tempted to do it anyhow. It's up to you to do the personal evaluation necessary to excavate these sources of disappointment in your life and to be really honest with yourself. The questions you ask yourself might include:

- What can I do to improve this situation or to get my needs met?
- Have I been led toward inaction by having this expectation?
- Am I outsourcing what I should do for myself, or expecting someone else to do it for me?

Let's be honest: it's very easy to love somebody who's doing everything you want them to do. It's all love, and that's a walk in the park. But if you really want your love to be tested, then deal with the moment they don't do what you want them to do. That's when you grow. That's when your heart expands, your mind expands, you expand, and you grow as a person.

EXPECTATION RESET

What do you do if you communicated your expectation and it was shot down? Or if you set an expectation with someone, but then they failed to live up to their side of the agreement? After you've tended to your feelings, what you do is find a way to reframe your expectation into one that actually can be set. This could mean asking yourself if there is someone else in your life who might meet it, or if you could meet it for yourself. In an article for *Psychology Today*, "6 Ways to Take Care of Yourself When People Disappoint You," Melanie Greenberg, PhD, runs through tips for attending to your feelings in the wake of an upset, then suggests some proactive ways in which you can still achieve a satisfactory outcome. She writes, "For example, if you have a plan to see a movie, and your friend cancels at the last minute, consider going by yourself. What other friends could you ask to come with you? . . . The important thing is not to give up and stew in passive resentment. Think about what a 'healthy adult' would do in this situation."

Greenberg also raises another important point. It's one thing when someone occasionally disappoints you by failing to meet agreed-upon expectations, but if this is a regular occurrence, you may need to rethink the relationship and its role in your life. As she points out, establishing and enforcing boundaries for yourself is an important act of self-care:

> Does it make sense to see this person less often or to keep the relationship more casual? Decide if this is someone you still want in your life, or whether your energy is better spent elsewhere. You may want to let the person know that you won't tolerate repeated broken promises, lies, or disrespectful treatment. Let them know what the consequence will be if they continue to mistreat you. Boundaries can help you feel emotionally safe, and they help restore your self-worth and self-respect.

Even if it takes some work to get there, let me tell you—once you have successfully set one expectation, and then another, and then still another, the benefits will grow exponentially. Use your words. From this day forward, never assume that someone magically understands or agrees to your expectations without you asking them first. It seems so simple, yet it requires practice. Why? Because it can be scary to express what you really feel or need. And the fear of rejection can be so strong, you might decide to remain silent. There's a scripture that says, "Life and death are in the power of the tongue." You must communicate what you expect—the quality of your life depends on it.

CHAPTER 5 **Expectation Examinations**

1. What is one expectation you need to communicate with someone about before you can set it?

    i. What is your plan for asking to have your expectation met?

    ii. What will you do if the other person can't meet your
        expectation?

2. If you were not able to set an expectation because you realized,
after communicating it, that it was unrealistic, is there a way to
negotiate with that person to make the expectation realistic? If not,
is there another meaningful, related expectation that you could set
instead?

3. Do you need to adjust the way you communicate with those in your
life, in order to be more positive and less critical?

4. Before you agree to an expectation from your spouse or someone
close to you, ask yourself:

- Why am I agreeing to this expectation?
- Who is it benefiting?
- Is this in my heart to do?
- What do I assume will happen if I say no, or try to renegotiate
  the expectation?

Part II

CULTURAL
EXPECTATIONS

6

DON'T DO IT FOR THE CULTURE, DO IT FOR YOURSELF

When a man is denied the right to live the life he believes in, he has no choice but to become an outlaw.
—NELSON MANDELA

As a man changes his own nature, so does the attitude of the world change toward him.
—MAHATMA GANDHI

All of us are impacted by cultural expectations every moment of every single day.

CULTURAL EXPECTATIONS ARE A SET OF BELIEFS, ATTITUDES, AND VALUES SHARED BY AN AFFINITY GROUP, SUCH AS A RACIAL, RELIGIOUS, PROFESSIONAL, OR SOCIAL GROUP.

As discussed, we are expected to think and behave according to our faith, race, gender, ethnicity, career, social status, and/or community. There is nothing negative about that expectation in and of itself. There are many cultural expectations I gladly adhere to. However, these are expectations I've chosen and set for myself. It's okay to meet any of the cultural expectations being asked of you, as long as you choose to do so. One of the most challenging aspects of cultural expectations is that they can be difficult to untangle and set, because of how deeply ingrained into our psyche they may be, and that can be damaging.

Think about it: How much of your current inner turmoil is being compounded by what is expected of you by your culture, your family, your church, other members of your gender, and others of your race? Not to mention how much pressure you put on yourself because of what *you* expect of yourself, based on the expectations of the culture?

Do you feel the pressure to live up to your parents' expectations? That's a cultural expectation. Do you feel the pressure to get a certain kind of job, by a certain age, or to earn a certain amount of money? That might seem like a professional expectation, but it could actually be a cultural one if the culture you are from puts a strong emphasis on professional achievement.

In my experience, cultural expectations are often the hardest and most painful expectations to shed. Sometimes, when we step back and are truly honest about what's in our heart, we're no longer able to just go along with our culture. Or sometimes, when we express our true self, we're no longer welcome within our culture. Ask yourself: *Do the cultural expectations I identify with actually match my personal values?*

It's important to keep in mind that cultural norms can and do change. We may believe these norms to be unchangeable truths, just because most people in our culture support them. But cultural norms are often created from opinions, as pointed out by Dr. Marie-Therese Claes in "Cultural Intelligence: Understand What Shapes Opinions." She wrote this article for *Psychology Today* in response to how she witnessed different populations addressing the coronavirus pandemic and the Black Lives Matter movement. As she points out: "If we have a culture, it means we share a meaning: the significance, the purpose, the value. Society is based on shared meanings; culture is shared meaning, the cement that holds society together. But society is not an objective reality, it is a reality created by all the people through their consciousness."

As Claes goes on to remind us, the fact that our culture is formed by our thoughts and beliefs makes us responsible for what we create. It also gives us the power to incite change, to cultivate inclusiveness, and to improve the tone of our culture at large. As she writes: "Cultural intelligence demands open-mindedness to alternatives—to the possibility that one's own views are false: everything is negotiable, nothing is sacred. Culturally intelligent people listen to each other's opinions, suspend them without judging them."

It's time for you to get fully aligned with what you value and the cultural expectations you set based on those values.

The process of setting a few carefully chosen cultural expectations for yourself, and releasing any that aren't actually true for you, may be disorienting. You may wonder who you really are and what you truly believe. But trust me, asking these questions is a necessary part of the process, and what's on the other side is the most incredible freedom you've ever experienced. Even if you've stifled your true voice for years, it's still in there, waiting for you to let it loose. And that's what we've been working toward in these pages.

I want you to shut out all of the noise from your family, your friends, your colleagues, your church, your social media feed, or wherever else the noise is originating from in your life. We are all too aware that, unfortunately, most of the groups we belong to will make us think we're crazy if we go against their widely shared beliefs. As a result, we usually give in to the pressure to conform our belief system to our culture's and do what's expected of us, even if it's not in our heart. While we know that the price we must pay to live according to these expectations is extremely high, the idea of being at odds with our cultural groups is so terrifying that we do it anyway.

ARE YOU GOING TO BE SOMEONE YOU'RE NOT FOR THE REST OF YOUR LIFE, JUST TO BE ACCEPTED?

Rather than feeling dominated and suffocated by the expectations of others, what if you created the standard by which you live? Not by trying to convince anyone that they are wrong, but by having the courage to set your own expectations and live only by the ones you choose. You must take an active role in creating the life you want, and changing what you don't like in your culture starts with you.

CANCELED?

Our fear of being rejected by various cultural groups has taken on an even more ominous tone with the rise of "cancel culture," which has become a pop culture catchall term for any behavior deemed unacceptable.

According to the *Merriam-Webster Dictionary*, "to cancel someone . . . means to stop giving support to that person. . . . The reason for cancellation can vary, but it usually is due to the person in question having expressed an objectionable opinion, or having conducted themselves in a way that is unacceptable."

The wrath of cancel culture isn't just reserved for celebrities or pop culture personalities. If a private individual says something, does something, or posts something the cancel culture doesn't agree with, then it employs a variety of tactics—from public shaming to social ostracizing—that can have widespread negative consequences for that individual. Depending on who you are, you're supposed to say (or not say) and do (or not do) certain things, or you will get "canceled."

For example, if you see that a majority of your cultural peers have posted about a subject online, you might think, *Well, if everybody else is doing it, I'd better do it, so nobody says anything about me.* It may not be in your heart to post anything, but you're like, *You know what? I'm going to go ahead and do it anyway.* It just seems easier to go along with the expectation, but just going along with an expectation can be a slippery slope. President Barack Obama acknowledged the problems inherent in cancel culture when he spoke at a summit in October 2019: "This idea of purity, and you're never compromised, and you're always politically woke, and all that stuff, you should get over that quickly."

The negative impact of cancel culture has been widely debated for some time now. In the summer of 2020, 153 well-known artists and intellectuals—both conservatives and liberals—signed a letter published in *Harper's* magazine titled "A Letter on Justice and Open Debate." Here's a thought-provoking excerpt from the letter:

> The free exchange of information and ideas, the lifeblood of a liberal society, is daily becoming more constricted . . . [including] an intolerance of opposing views, a vogue for public shaming and ostracism and the tendency to dissolve complex policy issues in blinding moral certainty. . . . As writers we need a culture that leaves us room for experimentation, risk taking, and even mistakes.

If you're fearful of being shamed on the internet, or elsewhere, for your beliefs or for your refusal to go along with certain cultural standards, there's a good reason you're feeling this way. Yet, I continue to maintain that in the midst of so much trouble and friction, we must hold true to our own beliefs and standards, speak and behave in ways that are authentic to us (as long as they don't cause harm to others), and set our own expectations with the same respect and compassion for ourselves that we show to others.

We don't control anyone's thoughts or actions any more than they control us, but we can go far by demonstrating our own self-control.

In terms of social media, even if a topic is sensitive for you, don't raise your voice or resort to sarcastic or mean comments online. Set a different tone in your own social media posts and in your conversations with members of your family and cultural groups—a tone of acceptance, mutual respect, and inclusivity. Use conciliatory comments like, "I respect your right to your opinion, and I choose to see it a different way." Even small, seemingly insignificant actions like this are how positive cultural change begins.

It's not always your responsibility to justify your beliefs or lifestyle to others. Of course, not everyone will choose to follow your lead. But by being positive and proactive, you can help reset broader cultural expectations to be more inclusive. Believe in your own, and everyone else's, right to be free. You'll be taking the first step in creating space for that freedom in your life, not just for you, but for everyone you care about. Ask yourself:

- Do I need to pull back from social media or any cultural groups I identify with, at least for as long as it takes for me to set my own cultural expectations for myself?
- Have I allowed anger or fear to cloud my interactions with anyone in my life?
- Could I change the tone of these interactions so as to model compassion and inclusivity?

IT'S YOUR LIFE TO LIVE

The *Los Angeles Times* reported in April 2018 that teenage suicide rates were on the rise, and that 12.8 percent of adolescents aged twelve to seventeen (or 3.1 million kids) had experienced at least one major depressive episode, according to the National Institute of Mental Health. Experts pointed to two causes for this jump in unhappiness, which had been found equally across different races, ethnicities, and social classes. The first was social media, and the second was the increase in the intensity of the pressure kids were feeling on all fronts. As Patrice Apodaca wrote in the piece:

> Far too many kids today are feeling extreme levels of stress and anxiety because of exaggerated expectations—by their parents, their schools, their peers, and perhaps most crucially, by themselves—of accomplishment in academics, sports and other activities. The pressure to be "perfect" appears to be driving acute feelings of failure and hopelessness.

The fact that the strength and prevalence of cultural pressures have led to an increase in depression and suicide is alarming. As we've discussed before, I understand this pressure deeply, as I've struggled to shed my own "Mr. Perfect" expectation.

The pressure to live up to what others expect of us can be intense, especially when we look at how this plays out within our families. These are the people we usually love the deepest and rely on the most (even if we don't always agree with them). Moving away from their expectations of us might be complicated and scary, but it's necessary if those expectations don't suit us.

I've navigated this complicated process myself and have the emotional scars to prove it. Having grown up as a Black Christian man, I know all too well how many expectations can be put on a single person by family, community, and the culture at large. For example, there was an expectation that I was going to go to Oakwood University in Huntsville, Alabama. Although I grew up across the country in Oakland, California, my mom, younger brother, aunts, cousins, uncle, and many in our Seventh-Day Adventist church community had gone to this school. I could feel the weight of what my family and my home church (Wings of Love Maranatha Ministries in Oakland) expected me to do. But I knew in my heart that I could not go to Oakwood and be happy. It was not what God put in my heart.

I knew I was supposed to pursue a career in Hollywood, so I needed to go to school in Los Angeles, where I would have ample access to internships and job opportunities that would help me get my foot in the entertainment door. And I also knew if I bowed to the pressure to go to school in Huntsville, I might miss out on the life I felt called to live.

It's okay to value the opinions and feelings of your family, but do you value your own opinions and feelings more? It brings tears to my eyes when I think about how many people ultimately give up the life they were supposed to live, just to satisfy their family. Don't do this. Resist the temptation to make this exchange.

LOVE YOURSELF ENOUGH THAT YOU DON'T ALLOW YOUR FAMILY TO BECOME YOUR GOD.

There's a beautiful, amazing, and adventurous life for you, and I encourage you to live it, even if doing that puts you at odds with the people you love the most.

Gathering the courage I needed to go to the school I chose, not the school of my family's choosing, was a matter of listening to my spirit, which was saying, *No. That college is where they want you to go. It's not where you want to go. That's not you. That's their desire. It's not yours.*

Once I knew what was true for me, I also knew that I had to speak up for myself. I did just that and ended up attending my preferred college, the University of Southern California. I didn't let myself buckle under the pressure of others' hopes for me. Even though I cared about them and their opinions, I cared about mine more. I went my own way, and I accepted the consequences for my decision. I made the right choice, and instead of allowing them to define my life for me, at the expense of my happiness, I'm living the life I was called to live.

IT'S YOUR LIFE TO LIVE. DON'T LET ANYONE ELSE LIVE IT FOR YOU.

There are a lot of shades of gray when it comes to family relationships. For some, there are places where they basically agree to disagree with their family, whether it's about politics, or religion, or how they're parenting their own children. That doesn't mean they don't love and respect their parents and siblings. It just means that they have looked deep within themselves and acknowledged that, in order to be true to themselves, they are going to have to make some choices that work for themselves.

Life coach Paula Jones made these types of choices when she finally declared her independence from her parents, a decision she describes in her essay "Breaking Free from Your Family's Expectations," published in *Tiny Buddha*. She admits to having been rebellious in her youth, but her adult independence was not about trying to push back against her parents. It was actually an attempt to get closer to them, while staying true to herself.

As an adult, she acknowledged how important her family was to her; she loved them. She wanted to have a healthy relationship with them, while charting her own course in life. So, rather than resenting them, she put her energy into communicating who she really was to them. As she describes it: "I shared with them my conscious decision while I stood in the fire of their adverse opinions and reactions. Standing in the fire means I held on to my desire and my love for family while I faced down their criticism. . . . I was able to stand there and let their criticism and opinions wash over me while remaining in a loving space."

As Paula makes clear, her parents' initial reaction was not a positive one. But because she was able to hold tight to her two truths—that she loved and respected her family, and that she loved and respected herself enough to fight for her right to be independent and happy— she was able to weather this rocky period, until they finally were able to accept her true self.

I know that, unfortunately, such a reconciliation will be impossible for some people. No matter how carefully you plan your interactions with your family, or how much love you bring to the endeavor, they will not be able to accept your true self or lifestyle. If these are the circumstances in which you find yourself, my heart and prayers are with you. But I still maintain, and will always maintain, that independence is worth it—no matter the cost.

"Familyships" can be complicated, but if your will clashes with your family's will, are you really going to put their joy over the joy of living your own truth? If you've done this time and time again, maybe that's why you're so unhappy right now. You can make a different and better choice, starting now.

FOLLOW YOUR HEART, NO MATTER WHERE YOU'RE FROM

Another example of the delicate but workable balance between generations who see the world differently is the relationship between immigrant parents and their children. Often, these children must straddle both the expectations their parents bring from their homeland culture and the modern values of their new homeland, which feel more natural to them.

For my good friend the Nigerian-American comedian Yvonne Orji, who broke out playing the sidekick to Issa Rae's protagonist on the popular HBO show *Insecure*, these issues are clearly close to the surface, in both her life and her comedy. When she released her debut comedy special on HBO in June 2020, she titled it *Momma, I Made It!* She told the *New York Times*: "You don't get to be Nigerian and tell your parents you want to do comedy without getting a couple of degrees under your belt first. . . . Those are the rules. After I got my master's degree, I knew I didn't want to go to med school, but I didn't know what I wanted to do, either. Really, it was God who told me to do comedy, and I was like, 'OK, I hear you.' "

Even though Yvonne has had the courage and conviction to follow her passion into the career that God called her to pursue, she confesses that she still wants to make her parents happy, and not just in some version of her own happiness, but according to their cultural expectations: "Growing up as a child of immigrants, you're raised to be community focused; you never forget home. It's a never-ending quest to make your family proud. And while I've achieved a level of success at this point, I still want to buy my parents a house, or show up to the village with a car."

As America becomes more and more of a melting pot, we are seeing more varied representations of all different types of assimilation. Just take comedian Aziz Ansari's Netflix comedy series *Master of None*, which drew on his own experience of feeling like he'd disappointed his Muslim parents, who are natives of India and play themselves on the show. He even devoted a whole episode to a plotline about his parents wanting him to pretend he was still a practicing Muslim, to keep up appearances for his aunt and uncle during a family visit. After he's blown the charade by ordering pork at dinner, he and his parents have a confrontation in which he explains the difference between their two generations and why he's done pretending:

> AZIZ (AS DEV): Look, I get it. For you guys, religion has its cultural value. It's not like that for me. It's people calling me terrorist and getting pulled out of airport security lines.

Aziz acknowledges that he's wrestled with the issue. In a 2017 interview with NPR's Terry Gross, he sums up where he's come out on the issue this way: "I don't know what the answer is. The answer I kind of came to in my own life and in the episode is just, you know, there's a difference between respecting your own values, and there's another thing of just rubbing it in someone's face and maybe hurting their feelings."

Aziz wrote a moment into the show that represents how he and his parents eventually moved toward greater mutual acceptance—they would come to terms with his not being as religiously observant as they were, and he would not disrespect their beliefs in front of them.

YOU HAVE TO PAY THE BILL

My wife, Meagan, has an associate who once posted this profound observation on Instagram:

> One of my biggest lessons: Stop putting expectations on people that they didn't ask for. HARD TRUTH—I spent SO MUCH TIME being disappointed in, by and with people. Then one day I realized, it was MY FAULT. I put expectations on people that 1) they didn't ask for and 2) that oftentimes were incapable of fulfilling because it wasn't in

them. . . . And I knew this. Yet, I still did it anyway. So to
save some others grief, I implore YOU to stop too. People are
who they are. Pure and simple.

These words ring so true. What I've learned through all of my work
around expectations is that I'd rather see you disappoint somebody
else than disappoint yourself by not being who you really are. That's
a very important rule, although it's probably contrary to what you've
always been taught.

Our spirit keeps a tab, just like a credit card company does. We
may not be completely aware of what's on the statement. We kind of
know, *Well, I bought some shoes. I bought those concert tickets.* But we
may not necessarily be aware of all of the details of our purchases,
and the full cost, until we eventually get our bill.

We're all running our own internal tabs, whether we're aware of
it or not. These unpaid tabs create resentments. Here's how it works.
Our subconscious keeps a detailed record of everything we spend,
emotionally and spiritually. The tab is always running, especially
when it comes to those things that are not in our hearts to do (even
if someone else wants us to do them). Not only do these resentments
build up, but the anxiety builds, the pressure builds, and the discomfort builds. We may not even be aware how much those negative emotions are building until the bill comes due. That's when we blow up.
We do something we can't believe we did. We say something we can't
believe we said.

Suppressing your true wants and needs, even for your loved ones,
will usually cause you to act out in unhealthy ways. If you look at
most of the dysfunctional behaviors in a family—for example, constant fighting, codependence, jealousy—I'd argue that you can trace
the behavior back to an unspoken resentment felt by the one doing
the acting out. Subconsciously, they were expecting something but
didn't get it, and now they're angry. Or there was something they felt

pressured to do, even though it really wasn't in their heart, and now they're mad about it. Ever been there before?

Learning to have an honest conversation about the original expectation, and then being real about whether it's possible to meet it or not, is actually way easier and less destructive than the explosive behavior that surfaces after a period of personal dissatisfaction or suppression. This is why it's so important to set expectations—to not just allow the circumstances to emotionally charge up your credit limit and then let it come due in a harmful way.

Here's an example: Let's say your mom loves to go to church. And she expects you to go whenever you're in town. But you don't like the church she attends. After a long, stressful week, the last thing you want to do is to cram yourself into a pew when you could be relaxing and catching the online service that you prefer. But she assumes you're going with her. And then the weekend comes, and she's acting as if you're going to go. She never stopped and asked you if you wanted to go, so you're mad, but she's oblivious to your rising temper.

And now you're resentful. Why? It's not really about church—it's the fact that your mom *expected* you to go, which made you feel like you didn't get a say in your own life. You don't want her to have the expectation that you're going to do all of the things she expects you to do, based on her desire for you to do them.

However, you do love spending time with your mom, and you want to make her happy when you can. And so, trying to be a good child, you go with her to church, even though it's not really in your heart. After church, you and your mom go out to eat and end up arguing over something small; the brunch is ruined, and now she's mad. By not telling her any of your ongoing resentments, you've subconsciously ruined the meal. Add up enough of these moments and the disconnect between you and your mom will grow.

In this example, it was your responsibility to jump off this resentment train as soon as your mom mentioned going to church. You could've said something like this: "Mom, I love you. I can't do that. I can't find joy in that. And I can't go along with it, simply because you want me to, because it's going to make me really miserable and resentful."

The best way to handle the conversation is up to you. But what I wouldn't do is go along with something that has not been discussed. Any and all expectations need to be discussed, and there needs to be clarity on whether or not you're going to agree to them.

As always, communication is key. While you don't control whether the other person's feelings are hurt, you can be as kind and respectful as possible. Your independence is not meant to hurt them, but to enable your own freedom. As is your decision to set any and all cultural expectations you choose to live by for yourself.

CHAPTER 6 Expectation Examinations

1. What are the top five cultural expectations you feel pressure to meet? Once you have listed them, organize them in order of significance or weight, from most to least important.

2. Where do you feel the most cultural pressure? From your family, your friends, your racial or ethnic community, your church, your work colleagues? What do you fear will happen if you deviate from what's expected of you?

3. How comfortable do you feel being your authentic self on social media? If you can't be yourself there, what other outlets for free expression can you cultivate?

4. What cultural or spiritual beliefs do your parents hold that seem out of step with your current life? Would you prefer to honor these beliefs, to show respect for them, or to go your own way?

7

FAITH: THE REAL SIXTH SENSE

Destiny is not for comfort seekers. Destiny is for the daring and determined who are willing to at times endure some discomfort, delayed gratification, and go where destiny leads.
—Bishop T. D. Jakes

I've been protected, I've been directed, I've been corrected. I've kept God in my life and it's kept me humble. I didn't always stick with Him but He always stuck with me.
—Denzel Washington

In the following famous moment from the Hollywood blockbuster *The Sixth Sense*, Cole Sear, a young boy, played by Haley Joel Osmet, reveals to Dr. Malcolm Crowe, a renowned child psychologist, played by Bruce Willis, that he can see what others can't: *dead people.*

> COLE SEAR: I wanna tell you my secret now.
>
> DR. MALCOLM CROWE: Okay.
>
> COLE SEAR: I see dead people. [. . .] They don't know they're dead.
>
> DR. MALCOLM CROWE: How often do you see them?
>
> COLE SEAR: All the time. They're everywhere.

Cole's learning how to use his ability to see the unseen is key to his success. So what does this have to do with faith? I love how Hebrews 11:1–2 from the Message Bible defines faith:

> *The fundamental fact of existence is that this trust in God, this faith, is the firm foundation under everything that makes life worth living. It's our handle on what we can't see.*

What we can't see is where our power lies. I have experienced this to be true.

FAITH WORKS.

I have witnessed firsthand the transformative power of faith in all areas of my life. At the same time, I'm sensitive to the fact that some of you reading this may not share my Christian faith—I understand and respect that, and I'm also here to tell you that faith can be the path to a deeper connection to yourself, your purpose, and your life. The good news is that real faith is all about setting spiritual expectations for yourself—the foundation of faith is having a relationship with the Creator of the Universe, God.

The amount of God's power we experience is directly related to our expectations of His power. In Acts 3:1–26, we learn some valuable lessons about spiritual expectations. In this story, the Apostles

Peter and John went together to the temple at the hour of prayer. At the exact moment they were walking up, a crippled man was being carried to the temple gate, which was called the Beautiful Gate; the man was put there every day to beg.

GET INTO THE POSITION OF FAITH

Right from our introduction to the crippled man, we glean valuable information. We are given details that can tell us about the expectations he probably did and didn't have on that day. He had been born lame, and because he had never been able to walk, he probably never expected to be able to walk.

Being unable to walk, he could not work, and so he had made a life for himself based on what his circumstances had always been. He drew on the compassion of people going into the temple, asking them to share what money they had with him so that he could survive. And so this day, as with all the days that had gone before, he expected what he'd always expected—*to receive a few coins to help him get by as best he could.*

As we've discussed, setting expectations is essential to living free. This is especially true when it comes to our relationship with God. Let's be honest: we can become very discouraged when it feels like we've prayed and yet our prayers have seemingly gone unanswered.

The great philosopher Aristotle said, "Nature abhors a vacuum." Which means that wherever there's a void, nature will fill it. The same principle applies to our thinking. When we aren't sure why our prayers haven't been answered, this lack of understanding creates a void. And we usually fill that void with negative thoughts: *It's never going to happen. I'll never make it. Why do I keep getting my hopes up, only to be let down again and again?* This inner voice can cause us to gradually lower our expectations over time, to the point where we only expect the bare minimum. Remember, Jesus said, "According to your faith be it unto you." So, when we expect the bare minimum, often we receive the bare minimum.

DON'T LOWER YOUR EXPECTATIONS OF WHAT CAN HAPPEN IN YOUR LIFE BECAUSE OF WHAT HASN'T YET HAPPENED IN YOUR LIFE.

Although what you're praying for hasn't happened yet, it doesn't mean it won't happen. What if I told you that your faith yesterday created your reality today, and your faith today will create your reality tomorrow? Here is the key to seeing your faith manifest:

LIVE LIKE WHAT YOU EXPECT TO HAPPEN WILL HAPPEN, EVEN BEFORE IT HAPPENS.

When you start to do this, you will see things in your life change in ways that will defy your logical understanding. One of the many amazing things about God is that He specializes in exceeding our wildest expectations. When you start to change your beliefs about what God can do, and the speed at which He can do it, you will see things manifest in a powerful way.

As you read this, you need to know that, just like there is mail on the way to your house, there are blessings on the way to your life, right this very minute.

YOUR BLESSING IS ON THE WAY.

All you have to do is to put yourself in the position of faith, and then stay in the position of faith, even when you might have good cause to be discouraged or filled with doubt.

THE POSITION OF FAITH IS A POSITIVE MINDSET.

It is expressed like this:

Everything is working out for me.
Nothing is happening to me; everything is happening for me.
No matter what happens, I will keep showing up with a positive
    attitude.
All things are working together for my good.
It didn't happen yesterday, but it might happen today.
I'm excited about who I am and where I'm going.
I feel like a blessing is on the way.
Today is the day when everything turns around in my favor.

As you practice staying in the position of faith, *the blessing will come to you.* Think about the crippled man, begging at the Beautiful Gate. What if he was too discouraged to sit there? What if he had stayed home that day, disappointed by what he had collected the previous day? Maybe he was tired of begging, tired of the judgment of others, tired of his lot in life. If he had given up, then he might have stayed home on that day. And he would have missed the blessing that was on its way to him, which was about to change his life forever.

If you stay in the position of faith, even when you're discouraged, the blessing you've been praying for will still be released to you. I know it doesn't always feel this way, even when you've properly set your expectations and released those that are unrealistic. There's a temptation to say, *What difference does it make how I live? What difference does it make if I show up for church? What difference does it make if I keep praying? What difference does it make if I keep reading the Word? What difference does any of it make? I've been doing it so long, and I've seen nothing change, so maybe I should stop what I'm doing, because it's not working anyhow.*

Maybe you think you've released all of your unrealistic expectations, but you're still holding on to one big one: your unrealistic expectation of what God's supposed to do, and how God is supposed to operate. I have seen, too many times, how this way of thinking can cause you to *not* believe anymore. Because you're expecting God to do all of these things for you. But faith is a two-way street. **You have to participate, even when you don't feel like it, or you won't see the results.**

EXPECTATION WITH NO PARTICIPATION EQUALS DEVASTATION.

You have to keep going to the temple gate every day. For you to believe that God is going to act in your life on your behalf, you must take responsibility for playing your part in whatever you want to bring to pass.

PARTICIPATION TAKES YOU TO YOUR DESTINATION

Anytime something's going wrong in my life, or not going the way I want it to be, I don't point my finger at God. I point my finger at myself. I stop and examine my process and ask myself:

WHAT AM I NOT DOING? WHERE AM I MISSING IT? WHERE AM I NOT APPLYING FAITH? WHERE AM I DOUBTING?

This is where people of faith all too often let themselves down. I cannot tell you how many times, in the church, I have heard something like this: "Well, I gave it to God. It's His will. He'll do it." And then, a few weeks or months later, I hear: "Oh, well, it's not happening. So, maybe it's not His will. Maybe it's not meant to happen."

To which I say, "Well, maybe not, but you really won't know unless you participate. On the other hand, it might be God's will, but you'll never see it, unless you do your part."

I do believe in "giving it over to God." But when I give it over to God, I absolutely do my part. And I trust that the results may not happen how or when I expect them to, but that they will happen.

For example, it has long been a deep passion of mine to have my own TV show, where I can help even more people by spreading my message of positivity and self-improvement through that medium. One of my first appearances on TV was in 2012 on Oprah's *Super Soul Sunday*. In the next year or so, I really clarified why finding a place for myself on TV was important to me: *I can be who I am. I can talk about what matters to me. I can bring all these different passions of mine together: entertainment, inspiration, motivation. I really enjoy doing it, and people respond to me when I do it.*

So, at that point, I really put it out there: "I want to be on TV."

And because I'd had that strong start, appearing with Oprah, this seemed like a realistic goal. Now, I have made many TV appearances since then, on the top shows on TV, from *The Today Show* to *Good Morning America*, but my own show has not yet manifested. However, I never let this delay make me question God's will. That's the wrong way to look at our faith. Too often, we try to get into God's business. What is God's business? God is in the business of How. We always seem to want to control the result, but remember: *the process is the result.* God says, commit to the process and keep putting yourself in position.

That's what I do, even when the opportunities I was hoping for haven't presented themselves to me. I continue to show up every day, committed to my process. I prepare myself for the very things I'm praying for. I know I don't control whether or not a television network thinks of me as a viable host. But I do control if *I* think of me as a viable host, and I control my ability to prepare myself for this new role.

I have consciously chosen to live a life where I consistently work on myself. I consistently develop myself. I consistently read. I consistently seek out mentors who can give me advice and perspective.

Even on the days when we are discouraged, or tired, or worried, even on the days when we have doubt in our heart, or we are feeling lazy, we have to get ourselves to the "temple gate" and into the position of faith. For the blessings you hope to receive, ask yourself:

- Have I allowed past disappointment to stop me from showing up in my faith?
- What are three things I know I should be doing to put myself in position in my life but haven't been doing, because I've become discouraged?
- How can I heal myself and be an active participant in my faith and my life again?

DON'T LIVE ON AUTOPILOT

Now, back to the Beautiful Gate. The crippled man had done his part by putting himself in position that day. But as you'll see, he was still only doing the bare minimum in terms of his faith. When he saw Peter and John about to enter the temple, he asked them for money.

Something fascinating happened next, something that reveals even more meaning for us:

"And Peter, fastening his eyes upon him with John, said, 'Look on us.' "

What is implied is that the crippled man was asking for money, maybe holding out his hand, without actually looking at the men to whom he was making the request. Even though his need was great, his lack of eye contact reveals that he was not asking with an expectation of receiving. This interaction suggests that he routinely asked for money, but with no expectation of receiving what he requested.

The crippled man showed up physically that day, but he hadn't *really* shown up mentally. Maybe he had allowed his past disappointments to seize his hope. It seems like he was only asking for money because that's what he'd always done. He didn't really believe there would be much of a payoff, and he certainly had no expectation of the blessing that was about to be bestowed on him.

Does this sound familiar? You may be guilty of going through life completely dependent on your routine, of simply going through the motions with minimal expectations. Too many people are on auto-pilot, never stepping off the perpetual hamster wheel of life. Living the same experience every single day without even thinking about it.

IT'S SO EASY TO LIVE WITHOUT REALLY LIVING.

You may even be checked out when it comes to your faith. You go to church out of routine. You pray because it's what you've always done. But you're not really communicating with God. You're not really asking: *God, where are you? What's really going on?*

Maybe your faith has become a routine, like any other cultural belief that's been put on you. You're feeling pressure to conform to the opinions or actions of those around you, especially if you were raised in the church. And while it's understandable to not want to upset your church family, remember, you are not living for them. You're living for God and for yourself. No one but you should set your spiritual expectations.

If we are stuck in a rut, God will allow problems to break up our routine. He loves us too much to see us squander our existence. You and I may never wake up from our routine otherwise. If problems don't come up sometimes—*How am I going to pay the rent? How am I going to survive when everybody's being laid off? How am I going to make it through this depression? How am I going to weather this breakup?*—we may never wake up.

God is a routine-breaker. Don't get me wrong: I'm all about having a good regimen, a solid process, and sticking to it. But we don't want to become so committed to our process that we end up living on autopilot, without thinking. It's like that situation I'm sure you've been in before when you're driving to a place you're so familiar with that by the time you've reached your destination you don't remember how you got there. You consciously checked out, and your subconscious took over. Can you imagine how many years of your life you could spend checked out? Doing things because that's what you think you're expected to do, but not actually living?

The good news is that you have already been called to wake up—to free yourself from the expectations that were holding you back in your life. And your spiritual calling will unfold as it is meant to, as with everything else you've already been building and working toward. Especially if you receive this message right now and start really looking at what's in front of you, at the blessing that is about to be given to you.

Sometimes when problems interrupt your life, it's because God is saying, *I need you to live. I need to wake you up, because if you don't wake up now, not only are you going to miss what's coming to you, but you're going to go in a direction I never designed.*

**I KNOW THIS MIGHT SOUND CRAZY, BUT I WANT
YOU TO THANK GOD FOR THE PROBLEMS YOU HAVE.**

GOD IS TRYING TO WAKE YOU UP.

WHERE ART THOU, GOD?

God was about to wake up the crippled man at the temple gate too. When Peter and John paused and spoke to the man, "the man gave them his attention, expecting to get something from them" (Acts 3:5).

They wouldn't have stopped if they didn't intend to give him what he expected, right? Well, actually, God had something even better in store for the crippled man.

"Then Peter said, 'Silver and gold I do not have.' "

So, they had the beggar's attention, but then they basically told him, "We don't have what you're expecting."

Why would God send a problem to break you out of your rut if He doesn't intend to give you exactly what you expect? To get your attention. And now that He has your attention, you will not miss what He is prepared to do.

YOUR PROBLEMS ARE THE PATH TO THE BLESSINGS YOU SEEK, NOT THE OBSTACLE TO THEM.

But in that moment, before the blessing was revealed, the man must have been crushed. He was focused on Peter and John; he was fully awake now, only to hear the message, "I don't have what you expect." He had broken free of the safe familiarity of his routine, only to be let down. It's easy to imagine how, in that apparent rejection, the man could have even questioned his belief in God.

Scripture says in multiple passages, "according to your faith, it will be done." Yet, I have a closet full of memories of praying for something that didn't happen. As a result, I'll be honest, at times I have questioned God. As a person of faith all my life, I've been taught to have great expectations, and that God can do things above anything I can ask or think. Well, after God repeatedly seemed to do less than I was asking or thinking, I had to ask the question that I'm going to ask you now: *Have I been expecting the wrong things from God?*

I know for some people asking this question might be controversial. But we must examine every place where we've possibly allowed unrealistic expectations to shadow our life and diminish our happiness. There is a real need to dig into this issue with honesty and humility.

We all can become despondent, finding ourselves in a place where we don't believe God is doing what He's *supposed* to be doing for us. Or where something we want isn't happening in quite the way we prayed that it would.

Sometimes it seems like we expect God to be a genie. We rub the magic lamp, we pray, and He's instantly going to grant our wishes. But going down this path of thinking sets us up for spiritual setbacks. God doesn't work like that.

We don't like it when we don't receive what we want, and we don't always process it in a positive way. That's why sometimes we become mad or frustrated, or even feel rejected. Even worse, we can find ourselves blaming God. We can say, "Why, God?" Or, "God fell short." In some severe situations, we might even question if there's a God at all. Our unrealistic expectations of God have caused us to have a crisis of faith.

Does any of this sound familiar to you? If so, this is the time to be honest with yourself about your expectations of God. Peel back the layers and ask yourself if there's anything in you, a resentment or a grievance, something you're holding on to because you really thought God was supposed to come through for you and He didn't.

Acknowledging what's inside of you is the first step toward releasing it, and healing yourself, so you can repair your relationship with God. First, as with any other area of your life where you've been let down, you have to start by clearing the space to grieve it. Maybe you were afraid to admit that you were mad at God because you didn't think that was okay for a person of faith. If you're having a real relationship with God, sometimes you're going to have feelings toward Him—just like with everyone else in your life. So let go of any guilt or discomfort that comes up for you and get in touch with the feeling you're having, whatever it may be.

Next, I'd encourage you to think about this relationship in a totally different way—one without any expectations at all. I'm a Christian, but that doesn't mean I expect everything is always going to be great all the time. I understand there will inevitably be some things that happen in my life that I don't like. I might not even know why they're happening. I may have some ideas about what God is doing, what I can learn from it, but I don't always know why. I've learned to be okay with this.

It's easy to feel how the crippled beggar may have felt: *Okay, you've got my attention, and you're not going to meet my expectation?* Sometimes we allow our disappointment to overcome us, not realizing that God has the best plan for us, in the long run, even if we are upset today. Remember, your story is not over. Resist the temptation to let any setback you may experience take away your faith.

SEE WITH GODLY VISION

Before we look at the blessing that God bestowed on the beggar, I want to point out another aspect of this story that has always struck me. It is the fact that God, acting through Peter and John, chose to deliver a great blessing upon this man in the first place. God chose him to be a powerful example of expectations. This man had no idea his life would eternally play a significant role in displaying God's power.

The man may very well have been dirty and disheveled. He was poverty-stricken and couldn't provide for himself. But there is no clause in God's Word that says you only receive His blessings if you have a professional position, or if you look a certain way, or if you're employed or unemployed, successful or a failure, rich or poor. God is love. His love is universal, as are His blessings.

This is a message that could bear repeating in many communities of faith, which can sometimes be extremely judgmental when someone doesn't fit their limited idea of what it means to be a Christian.

What we see in this story is that anyone can be used by God and become a good example for us to look up to. A powerful representation of this in contemporary life is my good friend Sarah Jakes Roberts, the daughter of Bishop T. D. and First Lady Sarita Jakes, and wife of one of my best friends, Pastor Touré Roberts. After growing up in the public eye of her father's Dallas church, she forged her own path, taking some heat along the way because it didn't resemble what many people thought a Christian path should be. She courted controversy when she gave birth to her first child at age thirteen. And again when she married an NFL player at nineteen, which led to the birth of her second child at twenty and a divorce by twenty-three.

But all the while, Sarah was developing her own unique identity as a Christian leader. She held her head up high as she grew into the roles of single mother and leader of the women's ministry at her father's church, a journey she revealed in her 2014 memoir, *Lost and Found: Finding Hope in the Detours of Life*. She has since expanded even further, stepping into the role, with her husband, of copastor at One Church Los Angeles.

She actually credits the troubles in her past for making her a more relatable role model for a new generation of young believers, as she expressed in an interview on *Get Up! Mornings with Erica Campbell*: "I think there's just this misconception that if you're Christian you have to look a certain way and act a certain way. So, I certainly stay within the Word of God, but my desire each and every time I get up to speak is to demystify this idea that you have to do it a certain way."

This is a great reminder that faith has many forms and that God can use us all as a dynamic demonstration of the power of faith.

EXPECTATIONS EXCEEDED

After the trials and tribulations come the blessings. Peter had first frustrated the beggar's expectations by telling him that he had no silver or gold for him. He went on to say this: "But what I do have I give you. In the name of Jesus Christ of Nazareth, walk." Taking the man by the right hand, Peter helped him up, and instantly the man's feet and ankles became strong. Peter didn't just tell the man to walk. He also gave him a hand up, lifting him from the ground.

At which point the man could be seen "walking, and leaping, and praising God" on his way into the temple. Everyone who saw him was amazed. They recognized the beggar, a man they had always known as crippled, and saw that he was now healed. He had completely defied their expectations by doing what they had never expected to see him doing—what he himself had never expected to do.

Now, if God had only delivered what the man had asked for—money—that would have paled in comparison to God's bigger plans for him: to allow him to walk for the first time in his life.

This is a powerful reminder for us to trust that God has a plan. We walk by faith, not by sight. Instead of allowing ourselves to become discouraged, or focusing on what hasn't happened, we need to start putting some faith into our talk. We need to say what is going to happen with the conviction of our faith:

I will be healed.
I will be whole.
I will be pain-free.
I will be generous.
I will walk in power.
I will become everything God has called me to be.

And here's the most important lesson of all: we don't know how long it's going to take. We don't know what form the blessing is going to appear in. That's God's business. But how you live, think, and feel is your business. Feel good about what's on the way to you. Think of the many great blessings you are going to receive. Live in the love of God and do your best to never leave it.

There have been many moments in my life when I've actually prayed to God to thank Him for *not* giving me what I had asked for, because the blessings that He bestowed upon me so exceeded what I had dared to pray for myself. We serve a God who specializes in exceeding expectations. Get ready for this abundance to happen in your own life!

CHAPTER 7 Expectation Examinations

1. What are the top five spiritual expectations you feel pressure to meet? Once you have listed them, organize them in order of significance or weight, from most to least important.

2. If you were raised in a certain religion, do its teachings or practices still speak to you? If not, do any of your friends practice a religion that feels more meaningful?

3. Have you ever tried talking to God? If not, why don't you try now? He's always there.

4. Was there a time when you were disappointed but you can now see that God had a greater plan or blessing in store for you later in your story?

5. Is there something you are expecting or hoping for that you could give over to God? What is your part in this process? What do you need to work on to make this happen?

8

GET YOUR HOPE BACK

I learned working with the negatives can make for . . .
better pictures.
—DRAKE

Keep hope alive.
—REVEREND JESSE JACKSON

We've discussed all of the ways that expectations are driving us crazy
and stressing us out, putting too much pressure on us to live up to
what we expect of ourselves, what we expect of others, and what others expect of us. We've also talked about how this is what we've been
raised to do—to believe we'll be happy only when we earn that A,
lose those ten pounds, or earn that certain number of likes on that
picture we posted. Those are only some superficial examples of how
this insidious way of thinking operates. That's why I wrote this book:

I saw a profound need to help all of us completely transform our lives and live free by learning to set our expectations.

I want to pause for a moment. I've called you to do a real personal reckoning in these pages, confronting baggage from your family, culture, and peers, and to acknowledge the ways in which you may not have always stayed true to yourself. As I've shown you, we all have work to do in this department. But it's never too late to start, and even small steps can lead to big rewards. It's important to remember to do this work from a place of positivity.

If you're like me, then I know you've endured some difficult challenges in your life. It's probably been hard sometimes to find a reason to keep hoping when so many of your prayers seemingly haven't been answered. I feel your pain.

However, I want you to trust me and believe me right now when I say there is always a reason to have hope. Hope is necessary to our survival. If an artery in your heart is clogged, it has to be cleared; hope functions the same way. If you're not feeling hopeful, you have to unblock your hope. Your life depends on it.

This is why having some carefully set expectations is essential. Expectations serve as our hope valve. Think again about the heart. If any one of the four heart valves—tricuspid, pulmonary, mitral, and aortic—doesn't open properly, life-threatening problems can develop. Just like a heart valve, if our hope is turned off, the results are devastating emotional, spiritual, and physical problems.

Simply put, we need hope to survive. We are driven by hope. We are created for hope, period. If we don't have it, we're not going to even be able to climb out of bed in the morning. (Ever been there before?) We've all had periods of nonclinical depression. Everyone knows how it feels when you don't have enough hope that things will turn out right to motivate you through the day.

This is why I always answer the same way when I'm asked:

GIVEN THE CHALLENGES EXPECTATIONS CREATE— WOULDN'T IT BE EASIER TO DO AWAY WITH THEM ALTOGETHER AND LIVE WITHOUT EXPECTATIONS OF ANYONE OR ANYTHING?

No. Why? Because we can't live completely without expectations for one reason: *hope.*

At the same time, we can't let our hope run wild. Expectations are like blood pressure—they have to be managed in order for our lives to function successfully. And while expectation is dependent on hope, not all expectations are created equal. Only when we learn to manage our hope can we unleash its immense power to make our lives fulfilling.

Here's what healthy hope looks like: hope keeps you motivated, it keeps you upbeat, and it keeps you from feeling stressed or overwhelmed. That's why this work is crucial. When your expectations are properly set, you're optimistic, so that even when your expectations challenge you, it will be in a productive way.

The power of hope was made clear to Dr. Dale Archer, a psychiatrist and the author of the book *Better than Normal,* when he worked with survivors of Hurricanes Katrina and Rita. In an article for *Psychology Today,* he explained how those who managed to maintain their hope, no matter how much they had lost, were more resilient than those who had become passive and pessimistic: "Hope is the belief that circumstances will get better. It's not a wish for things to get better—it's the actual belief, the knowledge that things will get better, no matter how big or small."

The challenging part, of course, is that bad and unexpected events—like Hurricane Katrina, like the Covid-19 pandemic of 2020—can snatch our hope from us. Although it can be hard to find hope when it feels like the walls of your life have caved in on you,

you've got to pull yourself back up, dust yourself off, and find something you can believe in again. Hope is necessary to make it through the darkest of times.

THE DEVASTATION OF DISAPPOINTMENT

Let's go a step deeper:

ARE YOU FEELING HOPEFUL?

If you answered yes, then great! You can skip ahead to the next section. (Just kidding.) But if you answered no, keep reading. If you aren't feeling hopeful, maybe you are still nursing a disappointment, probably about an expectation you hadn't properly set, and that disappointment ran aggressively over your happiness.

Whether it's in life, work, love, or money, nothing steals hope faster than disappointment. The pain of past letdowns can keep you from moving forward. It's vital to detect the sources of any such lingering pain and work to resolve them. That way, you'll free yourself from your old baggage, producing a clean slate for your spirit and an unburdened heart as you set healthy new expectations for yourself.

In order to resolve your hurt feelings, you have to figure out whether you require an internal or an external resolution. For example, let's say you're upset that you didn't land the job you wanted. The only way to resolve that feeling is to do so internally and make peace with it. But let's say one of your friends frustrated you. This could require an external resolution: speaking your truth to that friend.

In my experience, most disappointments need an internal resolution. And one of the reasons we experience them in the first place is that our expectation wasn't met. If you're really being honest as you read this, you may have to admit you're grieving a loss—of an opportunity, a relationship, a friendship. You can heal yourself by bringing attention to your grief. Stop trying to power through it. That won't work. Admit how devastated you were by the loss, and maybe still are, even if it's been years since the initial upset.

Devastation comes in all shapes and sizes:

- Someone cheated on you. Now you're with someone good, but you don't trust them.
- The person you love didn't want to marry you.
- You're a certain age and you're not married yet, even though you expected to be.
- Growing up, you were overlooked by your family.
- You expected to be promoted at work, but instead they fired you out of the blue.

We face an innumerable number of hurtful scenarios in life. Your pain is going to look different from everyone else's—including the pain of others in your family or in your relationships. But I've got a proposition that I believe is the key that will unlock and release your pain: **The more you heal today the more your future self will thank you tomorrow.**

We all have scars from having our expectations disappointed. All we have to do is pull up the memory of just one of those disappointments and it feels as if it happened yesterday. If you want to take a step toward healing, ask yourself:

- What was the most painful hurt I experienced? Why was it so devastating?
- What do I need to do to forgive the person who hurt me (if another person was involved)?
- Does removing the expectation I had of the person or situation that let me down give me a different perspective that allows me to heal?

It is totally within your power to live free right now. In order to do so, however, you must finally tend to old wounds so you can move forward and embrace the present moment with greater hope. That will also make you better able to assess others and situations for what is and isn't realistic to expect from them, as we've discussed.

I know this process isn't easy, but the quality of your future depends on it. Now is the time. You're not reading this book by accident; you are reading it right now by divine appointment. God is showing you that this pain is holding you back, crippling you emotionally, mentally, spiritually, and even financially.

Let's say you came to me and told me: "I can't get over it."

This is what I would say to you: "You can't *not* get over it!"

Perhaps the pain of an unmet expectation is triggering a deeper trauma from your past. If that's true, then you may need to go back even further in your self-work and deal with that original experience. You may need support to do this. There can be great benefit in seeking the help of a therapist, counselor, pastor, life coach, addiction specialist, or even a friend who has been through something similar and can really help you work on healing. Whatever solution may be available, seek it out now. Don't allow the pain to linger any longer.

If there is no deeper trauma tethering your pain, my question isn't "Why can't you?" but instead, "Why *won't* you?" If you have the ability to do something and yet you're not doing it, you're making a choice— even if it's a subconscious one—to stay in the pain of that past hurt rather than work through it and commit to rejoining your life today.

What's keeping you stuck in the past? Ask yourself:

- Am I afraid of unknown experiences in my future?
- Is it easier for me to hold on to the hurt because it's a more familiar feeling than the unknown feeling of healing?
- Is this way of thinking or feeling just a bad habit that I don't need anymore?

As with all of the self-work we do around setting expectations, there are no wrong answers to these questions. All that matters is that you are really honest with yourself. You may have to give yourself a good talking-to—you may have to say: *Is my hope for the future and my desire to have the life I want greater than my commitment to the pain I've experienced?*

Hopefully, your answer is absolutely *yes*.

Letting go of pain will not only set you free but also allow you to see the situations and people in your life today for what and who they really are. This is why releasing upset around expectations is so powerful—and necessary—in order to make more room for hope.

GOTTA HAVE HOPE

If this message is resonating for you right now, ask yourself:

- What am I allowing to take my hope?
- What would help me cultivate more hope right now?

Your hope expands when you can gain mastery over the aspects of your life that are actually within your control. I equate the word "hope" with expectancy. Expectancy is optimism—the idea that it would be *nice* if what you want happens, but it's okay if it doesn't.

Hope is a critical element of happiness and success, as important as discipline, focus, determination, and persistence. When I've lost my hope, it hasn't taken me long to realize I can't function and need to find another way. In the days of rebuilding my self-confidence and pivoting in my career, it became a personal challenge for me to figure out how all of this worked. As I often do, I started with a series of questions to try to find the best, most useful path forward, and I encourage you to ask yourself these questions as well:

- Is my hope full or low? How much do I have?
- What am I hoping for?
- What in my life is bringing me hope right now?

Even now, I still return to these questions again and again. They help me to constantly assess, prioritize, and, when necessary, pull back.

Hope is necessary to weather the little bumps in the road we encounter every day, and it's especially crucial when life takes a turn for the difficult or becomes downright devastating—as it did for so many people during the pandemic of 2020. But hope is not a cure-all. It can actually become detrimental when we become obsessed with tying it to a specific desired outcome that must occur on a time line we've determined.

Linzi Clark wrote a simple but instructive personal essay on hope, "How to Survive Hard Times: 5 Lessons from Volunteering in a Hospital," following a stint as a volunteer in a ward of patients who had suffered catastrophic spinal injuries that left most of them paralyzed. As she came to see during the time she spent with these patients, it was important for them to have hope that their condition would improve in the future, especially through all of the painful and difficult physical therapy and rehab.

But she also saw that when patients set unrealistic goals for themselves, their hopes flagged and they ended up feeling discouraged. From this observation, she drew some advice that is pertinent for all of us, even those of us facing challenges that are much less daunting than paralysis: "Be patient. One of the most frustrating things about a spinal injury is not knowing how long recovery will take. . . . By not putting time frames on our expectations, we can simply observe the different learnings along the way and live more peacefully in the present knowing that we will reach our destination when the time is right."

As Clark points out, a better—and admittedly more difficult—

approach is to try to stay in the present moment and find acceptance there, because our response to the present is truly the only thing we can control. Yes, we should set both goals and expectations for ourselves and work toward them, but we should also allow our dreams and goals for the future to unfold as they need to. We can't dictate that they *must* happen by a certain date in order to be validated.

Our hopes can be extremely powerful, but we must stay mindful that they also can be very fragile, especially when we are attaching a time frame to them. For those of us who are very driven, this can be a challenge. Here are some questions to ask yourself if being hopeful has been a struggle for you:

- Is my impatience hurting my hope?
- What time line am I obsessing over and why?
- Is there a way I could adjust my process that would make me feel hopeful again?

THE INFORMATION PRESCRIPTION

A simple but profound way to cultivate hope is to seek out information on any topic that is causing you anxiety. Having more information will either help you have a more optimistic outlook or give you a needed reality check. A great example is the parenting how-to guide, *What to Expect When You're Expecting*. This book is so iconic that if you Google the word "expectations," it's one of the first things that usually pops up. The numbers on its cultural impact are staggering: it's read by 93 percent of moms-to-be who choose to read a pregnancy book, it has a perennial spot on bestseller lists, and more than 18.5 million copies are now in print. Not to mention that *USA Today* chose it as one of the twenty-five most influential books of the past quarter century.

Changing health-care trends and cultural norms since the book was first published in 1984 have created something of a backlash in recent years, as was examined by the 2005 *New York Times* article "Expecting Trouble: The Book They Love to Hate":

> Tracy Behar, the executive editor of Little, Brown & Company, a publisher of competing books, said she hated the book during her two pregnancies, finding it "scary and woefully out of date." But after her second child died of genetic problems at two weeks, she went back to *What to Expect*, wishing she had paid more attention to its warning signs, simply to prepare herself.

Conflicting opinions about the book's merits do not change the fact that women going through this major life transformation need a guidebook to help them navigate what's on the horizon. And while they may choose alternative sources of information that have sprung up in recent years, *What to Expect* remains a valuable resource for many.

Whether you're anxious about work, money, your health, or your future, at least some of that anxiety comes from a lack of information. While the term "fake news" has been thrown around a great deal in recent years and much unreliable and biased information is in circulation these days, especially on the internet, there are still good sources of information available. When seeking out books, magazines, and online publications on your own, try to read from several different sources, even if they offer conflicting opinions, as a way to achieve a broader perspective.

Most of our worries stem from an unknown outcome to a known problem. Anxiety erodes our hope, but the antidote is information. If you're concerned about something in your life, ask yourself: *What is the cause?*

For example, *I'm worried I won't be able to pay off my student loans.* Now figure out what is the unknown fueling your anxiety. *I don't know how I can ever pay them off, given where I am in life right now.* The unknown is: *How will I do it?* To move into a mindset of confidence and hope, overload yourself with productive information on practical steps others have taken to manage their student debt. Discover what you need to do to move yourself further along.

Being more informed will give you greater confidence to keep going, even in the face of your greatest challenges. You will feel more in control of the situation, and that feeling will help you have a more optimistic outlook and feel more hopeful.

Ask yourself:

- What source of good information could help me flip my anxiety to hope?
- How can I cultivate more hope by preparing myself for what comes next?

DARE TO HOPE

Another way to build more hope is to share the optimism you already possess (even if you don't have as much as you'd ideally want). In his moving, unflinching essay "The Machine Stops," the neurologist and writer Oliver Sacks wrote profoundly about the future, even knowing he was facing a terminal cancer diagnosis. After expressing his concerns about the many ways in which he had seen technology cause people to disconnect from the real world and from each other, he ends the essay, which was published in *The New Yorker*, on a remarkable note: "Nonetheless, I dare to hope that, despite everything, human life and its richness of cultures will survive, even on a ravaged earth. . . . As I face my own impending departure from the world, I have to believe in this—that mankind and our planet will survive, that life will continue, and that this will not be our final hour."

There's something so profound here about the inherent grace of letting go of his own expectations and replacing them with one belief for the world that will remain after he is gone. This is the power, against all odds, of daring to hope and sharing that hope. This is the power of what's possible when everything else is stripped away. How can we achieve some measure of this same power without the cost of a terminal diagnosis? By returning again and again to our hope—and by sharing it with as many people as possible.

We can do so in infinite ways, big and small. We can check in with friends and family members we know are struggling and encourage them with our experiences of perseverance. We can share our testimonies in a range of ways, from social media posts to volunteering. The good news is that hope grows exponentially, and there are infinite ways to share it. The more we cultivate hope in our own lives, the better able we are to help others cultivate it in theirs.

CHAPTER 8 **Expectation Examinations**

1. Is there an area of your life where you feel like you've lost hope?
   i. Write down five possible outcomes, and then arrange them in order of likelihood. Be honest and realistic. Don't let your fear run the show.
   ii. Even if the worst-case scenario happens, how bad would it really be? Is there anything you can do to avoid it?
2. Is there something that's due to happen in your life that's causing you anxiety? Is there anything you could learn or do to better prepare yourself so you can feel more secure about the likely outcome?
3. Are you allowing expectations about something negative that

happened to you, either recently or in the past, to interfere with your ability to move forward in your life?

4. Is there an area of your life where you've allowed your anxiety to override your hope? Can you move your perspective back to a place where, however nice a particular outcome would be, you're okay if it doesn't happen?

5. If you had one central hope, not just for yourself but for your children, or the next generation, what would it be? What can you do to contribute to the likelihood of this hope being fulfilled?

Part III

RELATIONAL EXPECTATIONS

9

IT'S NOT THEM, IT'S YOU

For me, the relationship journey has been very up and
down. But it didn't have to do with anybody else but me—
it was about me figuring out me.

—Jennifer Lopez

I blame movies for my high expectations in relationships.

—Anonymous

In August 2019, I spoke at one of the biggest relationship conventions
in the country, the Spark Marriage Conference at Lakewood Church
in Houston, Texas. I was there to help the thousands of couples in attendance recover the magic in their marriage. I was nervous because
I knew I had to reveal to them the truth about why their marriages
weren't working and share lessons I'd learned during some of the
roughest times in my own marriage.

I heard my message, loud and clear, in my heart and in my head. I knew it was important and potentially transformative. I knew that these people were the perfect seekers, ready to receive my message. After all, they'd had the courage to acknowledge that their marriage was in trouble and had come to the conference seeking a solution—or better yet, a breakthrough to save their marriage. I had so much respect for every couple in the room that had dared to be there and to live so transparently.

TRANSPARENCY LEADS TO TRANSFORMATION.

To achieve the transformation they sought, these couples would need to be more vulnerable than ever before. For the next forty minutes, I encouraged them to get real with me, and I promised to get real in return as I set out to help them fix their relationships. I started by telling them the problem wasn't with their spouse, but with them.

IF YOU HAVE A PROBLEM WITH YOUR SPOUSE, THE PROBLEM ISN'T YOUR SPOUSE.

THE PROBLEM IS YOU.

You could have heard a pin drop, it was so quiet in the arena. The silence let me know I had their attention. I went on to talk about how all of the issues in their marriage came down to one single word: *expectations*. *Their expectations of their partner were ruining their marriage.* The problem wasn't that their spouse didn't cook all the time, or take out the trash, or have the desired amount of sex with them. The problem was their expectations of who their spouse should be, and should behave—expectations they often had never communicated about with their spouse.

I explained that expectations are so powerful that they can change a great spouse into a poor one. *How?* Because expectations have the power to alter our perspective, skew reality, and distort our perceptions. These may seem like small effects, but they actually do the most damage in all areas of our lives, because they're at the root of most of our discontent.

For example, let's say your wife genuinely loves you. Her love can be completely obscured, however, by your expectations of her. Maybe you have an expectation that she won't stay glued to her phone when you eat together, and you've asked her many times not to do this. When your wife keeps her device at the table, your expectation of her isn't met, and you may misinterpret this behavior as indicative of a lack of love on her part.

You might think, *If she really loved me, she would put her phone away while we're eating together. She knows how much this bothers me.* Now, your wife might be showing you love in ninety-nine other ways, but because she has disappointed you in this one area, you become flustered and upset. At this point, there's a dangerous temptation to draw the incorrect conclusion about her actions and what they mean, because she didn't meet your expectations. Also, even though you did communicate your expectations, you didn't actually set them by securing your wife's agreement that meals will be a phone-free zone—and yet, you're holding her accountable anyhow, as if your expectation *had* been set.

Here are three critical steps in setting expectations in all relationships:

- Tell the other person what you expect.
- Ask that person if they can meet your expectation.
- Do not hold them accountable until they have agreed to your expectation.

ARE YOU ABOUT TO END IT ALL?

I also shared this important revelation with my audience at Spark: no matter how much we love our spouse, we are not God. We have to give our spouse the freedom to walk out their own relationship with God. We have to appreciate and respect that sometimes they're on a journey and all we can do is hold their hand while they go through it. We can't lead them along. We can't rush the process. They have to go through the journey themselves.

I asked the couples in attendance to look at themselves with real humility and honesty (as I'd had to do in my own life and marriage). And then, standing on that stage, in front of all those thousands of couples, I came right out and asked them a bold question:

"Is there anybody here who has been going through major challenges in your marriage, to the point where divorce has been on the table? I want you to stand right now."

Silence. In an arena with a capacity of 16,000, it was eerie. Then *bam*—just like that, couples all over the arena stood up. Seeing this public display of heart, vulnerability, and truth was one of the most powerful moments I've ever experienced. I prayed with them, declared victory over their marriages, and asked them to let go of the expectations that were destroying these marriages.

By the end of the night, multiple couples had sought me out to tell me that they'd almost instantly felt the stress of their marriage lift as soon as they released the heavy burden of their unset expectations, and that they'd decided to stay together. Talk about a powerful and healing reversal in their perspectives.

Nobody goes into a marriage thinking they'll end up divorced. Nobody wants to get divorced. It's a brutal place to be. But that's exactly where millions of couples end up every year. And it's an indicator of just how dangerous unset expectations can be.

If what happened at the Spark marriage conference resonates for you, ask yourself:

- What are three things I expected from my partner going into our relationship?

- Where did I get the idea that this was what a committed partner should do?
- Now that I really know my partner, and our relationship, was I being realistic?
- Did I ever ask my partner if they agreed to and felt able to meet my expectations?

If you are going through relationship troubles or trying to heal the wounds from a bad breakup brought on by unmet expectations, taking the time to answer these questions is critical.

THE MYTH OF THE PERFECT RELATIONSHIP

It's truth time—if there's one area where our expectations get us into the most trouble, it's around our relational expectations. We all know love is complicated, and we all have our relationship battle scars to prove it.

IF YOU HAVE RELATIONSHIP PROBLEMS, YOU HAVE EXPECTATION PROBLEMS.

Dr. Travis Bradberry, author of *Emotional Intelligence 2.0*, says this in an article he wrote for LinkedIn: "Your expectations shape your reality. They can change your life, emotionally and physically. You need to be extra careful about (and aware of) the expectations you harbor as the wrong ones make life unnecessarily difficult."

Your skewed reality can get even more distorted when there is another person involved, especially someone you love. As with all other areas of your life, you need to set your expectations about what you want and need from your relationships, and what you are willing to give in return. Before you can do this, you might need to dismantle some of the fantasies you have brought with you into adulthood, often without being aware of them.

Depending on your upbringing and your exposure to marriage growing up, as well as your own relationship history, you can come into a relationship, or even a marriage, with certain traditional ideals about how it's supposed to be. *The man is supposed to do this*, and *the woman is supposed to do that*. Then these ideals become unspoken expectations. Instead of asking your significant other how they want to divide up responsibilities, you act as if what you expect is obvious (when it's not). If your partner doesn't "measure up," then they are the problem.

In the most severe cases, relationships have been destroyed by ideals that became unspoken expectations. Think how different the outcome might have been if they had been spoken out loud. Maybe accord could have been found. Or not. But that's why we must learn to talk about it.

The problem is, it's possible to believe in your own ideals so much that if your partner doesn't do what you expect, you automatically make the judgment that they're a bad partner.

Really? Because your partner isn't obedient to your commands, now they aren't good? Well, no, as I told those brave folks who attended Spark, the problem isn't your spouse—*it's you.*

As pointed out in the PsychCentral piece "The Myth of the Perfect Marriage," we often shape our ideas of relationships on what we've seen on TV and in movies or read in romance novels. Even when we're old enough to know better, we don't stop to distinguish fact from fiction. Mary Laner, a professor of sociology at Arizona State University, has observed that most of us choose to blame our spouse for letting us down rather than admit that our expectations were unrealistic in the first place: "We think that our partner can meet all our needs, know what we're thinking, and love us even when we're not terribly lovable. When those things don't happen, then we blame our partner. We think that maybe if we had a different spouse, it would be better."

At Spark, why did this epiphany affect so many who attended the conference, so quickly, when nothing else they'd tried up until that point had seemed to work? Most people lack an awareness of all the relationship baggage they're carrying; they simply think that what they want or expect is the norm. Just as we discussed earlier about our personal expectations, our perspective is not reality, even though we often take it as such.

That night, by helping the couples at Spark observe the limitations of their own perspectives, I was able to immediately shift their mindsets to realize the error of their ways. And suddenly they saw their spouse in a totally new—and much more positive—light.

Many people have been married for decades without ever examining any of this. The consequences are usually friction and frustration—and sometimes much worse. At Spark, I shared with the couples the same good news I'm sharing with you—there is a simple fix to the problem. Take your unset expectations and see if they can be set by communicating them and letting your significant other respond. Once you have both agreed to the terms of an expectation, it can be set. Any expectations you can't come to terms on, you need to release, completely.

And if you're married and are so fed up that you're thinking divorce is the solution, did you know that, according to Professor Laner, the divorce rates for second marriages are even higher than they are for first marriages?

It's time to dismantle the fantasy you have brought into your relationship and build a realistic relationship that can support both partners instead. To do so, you've got to confront yourself about any unrealistic ideas you may be harboring. Ask yourself:

- When I recall my childhood, what images of marriage made an impression on me?
- What did I think a relationship looked like, based on TV, books, and movies?

- As an adult, do I think these qualities are actually realistic to ask of my partner?
- Can I recalibrate my fantasy so that "perfect" is the romance I'm in right now?

ONLY YOU CAN MAKE YOU HAPPY

We touched on this in chapter 5; now let's take a closer look at how our happiness functions. All of us are in a constant pursuit of greater happiness, every moment of every single day. One of the biggest mistakes we can make in a relationship is to expect the other person to be the source of our happiness.

YOU MUST BE RESPONSIBLE FOR YOUR OWN HAPPINESS.

When you outsource this responsibility to someone else, I don't care how much you love them, you are setting yourself up to be perpetually disappointed. No one is equipped to make you happy, twenty-four hours a day, seven days a week. It's an unrealistic expectation that weighs on so many relationships. And then we wonder why they don't work.

I need you to take full accountability for your own happiness right now and to stop putting that responsibility on the doorstep of your spouse or partner. When you don't shoulder this responsibility yourself, a crazy thing happens—you don't do the things that make you happy, and yet you expect someone else to do things to make you happy. Why would you expect someone to do something for you that you aren't even doing for yourself?

In a relationship, you can absolutely contribute to the happiness of your partner, and if you love someone you want him or her to be happy. However, there's a difference between *contributing* to someone else's happiness and *being the source* of their happiness. When someone says to me, "The person I'm with doesn't make me happy," it sounds as crazy to me as if they were to say, "The person I'm with doesn't make me money."

Most people have no expectation that the person they're with is supposed to earn money for them. So, if you wouldn't expect your partner to earn a check for you, why would you expect them to make happiness for you that only you can create?

A relationship or marriage is most often healthy when both partners contribute equally. When both partners or both spouses earn as much as they can individually, they have more to contribute collectively. "Contribute" is the key word. Can you imagine if each person took responsibility for creating their own happiness the same way they take responsibility for earning their own money? And then brought the happiness they'd created into the relationship? They would have more collective happiness than before. If couples practiced this, relationships would change for the better overnight.

I do believe that if you love someone, your main priority should be contributing to their happiness, and a "happiness contribution" from your partner is a realistic expectation to have. However, be careful not to mistake "contribution" for "creation." You and only you can create your happiness, and the same goes for your significant other.

LET'S TALK ABOUT SEX

A surefire way to contribute to each other's happiness in a relationship is through intimacy. I like to work out. I like to work. I like to spend time with my family. Sometimes my wife likes to do these things with me. Sometimes she likes to hang out with her friends instead, or do other things that I may not feel like doing with her. No problem. I can go to an event or a speaking engagement without her. I can work out without her. She can devote time to the things she likes to do without me. This expectation helps our marriage work—we don't pressure each other to do things that we like but the other may not. We both do this, and we can both honor our marriage in the process. As long as we have some common ground—some shared interests and some time that's devoted to the two of us—our relationship works. In fact, our time together is probably even better, because we've been rejuvenated by feeding our own interests.

However, if you and your significant other have made the commitment to be monogamous, sex is one activity you can't do separately. You have literally said, "I am committed to being your one and only sexual partner." If you aren't honoring your commitment—if you're not having sex with your partner—you're setting your relationship up for difficult challenges.

IN A MONOGAMOUS RELATIONSHIP, THERE'S ONE ACTIVITY YOU MUST DO TOGETHER: SEX.

This isn't a problem as long as the sex is flowing. However, when it isn't (which happens more often than people admit), it can be completely disruptive to your relationship. It's like you've made the commitment to be the only one who feeds your partner, your partner will be the only one to feed you, and according to your agreement, neither of you can go anywhere else to eat. Again, there's no problem with this agreement, as long as both of you feed each other. But what happens when you or your partner comes home, night after night, and there's no meal? You've made the promise that you won't eat anywhere else, and you're both committed to honoring that promise. But you both are still relying on each other for food that isn't being prepared. So day after day, you both get hungrier and hungrier.

I would in no way justify or excuse cheating, but when you understand it in this context, you can at least have compassion for those involved when it happens. You can understand why someone who's hungry would be tempted to eat wherever they can find food. And if they're really hungry, it's even more tempting to eat whatever food is put in front of them, even if someone other than their partner prepares it.

Again, I'm not saying anyone should step out of his or her marriage or monogamous relationship. What I'm saying is that this truth is critical to understand, so you can become more aware of setting the sexual expectations in your relationship.

In a relationship, we have a responsibility to affair-proof our union by addressing our partner's unmet hunger. When there is a sexual expectation that's not being met, it can be tempting to believe the only solution is to close up the kitchen—in other words, turn off your sexual desire. Or you can falsely think it will all just work out magically on its own. But if there's no process to address why the sex isn't happening and what can be done about it, you're setting your relationship up for potential failure.

For most people, when they're dating, there's usually no obstacle to having as much sex as they want. For some reason, though, when people get married, sex can often become an issue. I can't tell you how many couples have come to me and complained about this very thing. Why does this happen? I'd say that the expectations in marriage are greater than they are in dating. Remember I spoke about how expectations are weights? One of the reasons married couples struggle around sex is because they feel the weight of sexual expectations, and the increased pressure to live up to what their partner needs sexually can become a libido-killer.

FOR A SUCCESSFUL MARRIAGE, BOTH PARTNERS MUST BE SATISFIED BY THE AMOUNT AND QUALITY OF SEX.

The two of you have to set an expectation about how you're going to meet each other's needs in the bedroom so you can both be happy and fulfilled. Also, not always but often, your sexual life is indicative of what's going on in the rest of your marriage, so dismissing a sexual issue as "just sex" may be denying a deeper issue.

Few couples realize how expectations in general can hamper their sex life. Often their unmet expectations *outside* the bedroom are interfering with their desire to be there for their partner *inside* the bedroom. There may be unspoken resentments about other unmet expectations, or an overall disconnect may have crept in.

If you are experiencing this problem in your relationship, what I recommend is that you immediately work on setting, or re-setting, the sexual expectations between you and your partner. This starts with a holistic conversation about your expectations related to your marriage, both outside and inside the bedroom. Both of you should give each other equal time to talk, and the conversation shouldn't end until both of you feel heard and at least a few expectations have been agreed upon and set.

Here's a tip on what to do before that conversation ever happens. It actually applies to any difficult conversation you must have, but especially to one this sensitive:

WRITE DOWN WHAT YOU WANT TO SAY FIRST.

The issue of sex is such a vulnerable and deeply personal subject. When you're not getting your needs met, it can cause you to become very frustrated, and that makes it hard to communicate effectively with your spouse. As we know, it's never good to make any kind of decision out of negative emotions (like frustration or anger). Your decision may be rash, and you could end up regretting what you said or did. Having everything you want to say written down in advance can help you have a more successful and constructive conversation with your partner about your sexual expectations.

Here are some questions to help you figure out what you need to communicate:

- Do I currently feel sexually satisfied?
- If not, does my significant other know how I feel? Have we ever tried to improve the situation?
- What is one thing my partner could do (or not do) that would improve my satisfaction?
- Am I upset about something outside of the bedroom that makes me not want to have sex?

Set the tone for the conversation by being as gentle and loving as possible, and open the dialogue from a place of connection. Choose to establish a productive tone, along the lines of: "Okay, how do we figure this out? I love you. I want to work this out. Let's have the conversation and set some expectations we can both agree on." Then, no matter what your spouse says, even if you disagree or find it hurtful, do your best not to be judgmental. If your spouse has trouble identifying their own needs, encourage them to answer the questions above.

For every couple, the specifics of the conversation will be different, but here are some additional questions that might help you and your partner open up the topic and glean some valuable insights:

- Why are we not having sex?
- What do we need to do to start having sex more regularly?
- How could we make sure that both of us are enjoying our sex life more?
- How often do I think we should be having sex? How often does my partner think we should be having sex?

- If I want to have sex more often than my partner does, can we meet halfway?

It's not all about asking questions. As we've already established, if the reason you don't feel like having sex is related to something outside of the bedroom, say so now. Also, if you have not found your sex life satisfying for some time, help your partner by being specific: "Here's what I like. Here is what I don't like."

If this is an area where you are struggling in your marriage, I cannot recommend strongly enough going to see a sex therapist or a counselor. You can also pick up a book that will help you navigate this, like *Wanting Sex Again* by Laurie J. Watson or *His Needs, Her Needs* by Dr. Willard F. Harley Jr. Read the book together and talk about how it makes you feel and what it inspires within you.

What you absolutely cannot do is remain in denial any longer. You cannot continue to avoid setting sexual expectations that work for both of you.

DON'T BE AFRAID TO NEGOTIATE SEX.

As with all aspects of a relationship, some compromise is necessary for everyone to be happy. Your partner may say, "Hey, I want to have sex every day." That may be unrealistic, and you might reply by saying, "I can't do it every day. I want to do it once a week."

Whatever the specifics are, both of you have to work out the compromise so you both know what you can expect. If you set an expectation to which you both agreed, "Okay, once a week it is," and then it's not happening that often, you can hold each other accountable.

THERE CAN BE NO ACCOUNTABILITY IF
THE EXPECTATION ISN'T SET.

Before anything can improve, sexual expectations have to be set. Your marriage, your well-being, and your joy completely depend on it.

THE EXPECTATIONS OF "I DO"

If you don't want anyone to expect anything of you, don't get married. Period. End of story. You cannot go into marriage thinking that you can just go wherever and do whatever you want, without any consideration for your spouse. If you want to live completely free, then don't get married. When you decide you're going to open up your life to someone else and be accountable to that person, that commitment comes with responsibility and expectations.

For years, I've held on to a sermon from Bishop T. D. Jakes, on a VHS tape. (Remember those?!) He talks about how, when we get married, we don't really know what we're saying "I do" to. By the time we reach marriage, both men and women have many expectations of what it is. Then, in some ways, the reality doesn't meet their expectations *at all*.

In marriage vows, couples literally verbalize what they can expect from each other in marriage: "To have and to hold, through sickness and health, through poverty and wealth." When you say, "I do," you are saying, "I am going to be accountable to you. You are going to be accountable to me. We're going to walk this thing called life out together." It doesn't mean that each spouse doesn't still have their own goals and interests. But each is committing to an overall agreement of what can be expected in marriage for the rest of their lives.

MARRIAGE VOWS ARE EXPECTATION AGREEMENTS.

Whether you realized it or not, you've already vowed to meet certain expectations for your spouse, and your spouse for you. That's what it means to get married. However, the truth is, as soon as the wedding is over, the vows are usually forgotten. Going back over them, individually and with your spouse, can be a powerful way to recommit yourself to your marriage. And it's also a great way to talk about expectations as you discuss each vow and what it means for you, and what expectations it causes you to have. And then as you see how your spouse's feelings compare.

But the work doesn't stop there. Marriage vows usually only cover a general understanding of the marriage. That's the macro expectation. The micro expectations, and your specific expectations, also have to be set. For example, does the wife expect her husband to take out the trash? Or does the husband expect his wife to cook every night? Who's going to stay home with the kids? Who's going to pick up the kids from school or bring them to their activities? All those specifics still have to be worked out through discussion, not assumed. Sometimes married couples act as if somehow the other person is supposed to know their expectations and comply with them. How? *Telepathy?*

The anger you're feeling may be due to the fact that you haven't taken the time to explain your expectations, or to find out if your spouse agrees to meet them or not. After several years of regularly being disappointed, you might be fed up. That's understandable. But staying isolated in your anger and hurt is only going to take you further away from your spouse and the solution. Every couple needs to talk through their expectations. You'd be shocked at how setting expectations, together, can pull you back from the brink of divorce.

Yes, the hardest truth is to admit that the marriage you're in is not exactly what you expected or signed up for. Maybe you've been reading along in this book, and now your spirit is heavy. Honestly, you are not feeling all that hopeful about the chances for your relationship to survive. My heart goes out to you. That is a devastating realization. Pause. Breathe. It's okay. You can work through it. Look back to those brave men and women you met at the start of this chapter who attended the Spark conference. It was their willingness to acknowledge to each other that their marriage had gotten so bad that the thought of divorce had crossed their minds. It was that level of honesty and integrity that finally brought them back from the brink and started their healing and reconnection. If you've been afraid to admit that it's gotten this bad in your own marriage, don't be. In order to heal and to get it right, eventually you have to acknowledge that it hasn't been entirely working up until now.

And then you do the work. Yes, it's work, but it's the good kind of work—based on reality and communication. That kind of work actually has the possibility of leading to positive change and a better marriage.

DON'T GET MARRIED BECAUSE YOU'RE EXPECTED TO

Now, if you're in a committed relationship but you're not married, and you're feeling any concerns or doubts about that relationship, do not get married yet. Especially not out of an expectation that marriage *should* happen just because you're already engaged, or because you've been with this person for a long time, or because your parents are pressuring you. Giving in to any of those internal or external pressures is the worst possible thing you can do.

As we've discussed, marriage is a major commitment, and it's meant to be forever. If you have any doubts in your heart, save yourself and your significant other a whole lot of pain by walking back from a commitment until you feel better about the relationship.

It's okay to need a little more time before you decide to commit. It's okay to acknowledge that this person isn't your future spouse. Yes, it will be painful. Yes, it will cause upset in your life. But it's so much better to do that than to go into a marriage because it's expected of you, but not really in your heart. Too often, people think getting married will make their doubts go away or will magically fix their relationship. As you've seen by now, quite the opposite is true—once you get married, as joyful as it can be, that's when the real work begins.

EXPECTATIONSHIPS

Of course, marriage is far from the only area of our lives where we're guilty of all sorts of destructive magical thinking. We also do it with our work colleagues, friends, children, and even God. Evaluate any areas of your own life where you have been feeling frustrated by a person or situation. Ask yourself:

- Are my expectations realistic and communicated? Have they been set?
- If someone in my life is not honoring an agreement they made, have I confronted them about it?
- Can this relationship be saved, or do I need to take a step back for my own well-being?

Just like any other relationship, when two people enter into a friendship, they both have expectations about it—how much time they'll spend together, how intimate they'll be in their conversations, how likely they are to show up for each other when needed. And I've seen it so many times: someone who expects their friend to give exactly the same amount of time and energy to the friendship as they give. Well, that's an unrealistic expectation right there, and a recipe for resentment, especially if all of this happens inside of your own head and your friend doesn't even know what you expected of them in the first place.

Sure, you can have expectancy—you can hope your friend will give back as much as you have put in. You can think it would be great if they did. And yes, a sign of a strong friendship is when there's reciprocity, when it's a two-way street. But it might be that your friend has obligations—a family, a more demanding job, an elderly parent—that prevent them from giving as much to you as you've given to them. If this is the case, it's up to you to decide if this friendship is worth maintaining or not.

You may decide that, for the time being, it's okay if either you or your friend gives less. And it becomes a deeper friendship, because you don't feel taken advantage of. Or you may decide to find another friend whose life circumstances are more similar to yours, so you're more likely to have the same space in your lives for friendship.

But whatever you do, don't ever try to control someone else's behavior and not allow that person to be exactly who they are. It won't work, and it's not healthy for either person in the friendship. Rather than dismissing your friend as a bad friend because they didn't meet your unrealistic expectations, choose to see and accept them for who they really are. You don't even need to have a conversation with them to do so. You could simply acknowledge your feelings to yourself: *I'm disappointed. I wish we talked more often, but at least I'm glad that I can call him a friend.* Think about that. The moment you frame it from this more realistic perspective, you could make peace with that person you're mad at right then and there.

I do believe that what you sow, you will reap. Yes, being good, kind, and helpful are all positive qualities to cultivate—they will make you and your life better. But life is not some equation whereby you give a certain amount to someone and you automatically get that exact amount back from them. Yes, you will get back what you give—you will sow what you reap—but it might be from another area or another person in your life.

If you decide to talk with your friend in order to release your hurt feelings and hopefully improve the relationship, don't lead with what your friend *should* have done. Be up front about the fact that you are only operating from your perspective. Say something like:

"Hey, maybe I missed something. My expectation may be causing me to have feelings, but I want to talk it out with you. I assumed that, based upon how I've been there for you when you needed help, I could depend on you. And then, when I called you, I felt like you blew me off. I was hurt by that. Can you help me understand how you were seeing it?"

This is exactly the kind of conversation that can help you release any expectations that aren't realistic and replace them with expectations that are (which can then be set), and this will improve the overall health of any friendship you have.

Healthy friendships are an essential ingredient to a successful life. Identify any friendships that are toxic or have toxicity present within them and either work to heal them or work to prayerfully eliminate them.

CHAPTER 9 Expectation Examinations

1. What are your top five relational expectations? Once you have listed them, organize them in order of significance or weight, from most to least important.

2. What have you been blaming on your partner that you now see was really a problem created by your unset expectations?

3. If you have been living in resentment within your marriage, can you forgive your spouse?

4. If you could ask your spouse to make one change, what would it be? Is it a realistic request? If your expectation is realistic, set aside a time to have a conversation about it.

5. If you have realized that you need to take serious steps to save your marriage, what's one thing you could do to move this process

forward? For instance, could you look for a marriage counselor? Or write down the main expectations you need to communicate with your spouse about?

6. If you have realized that you are in a relationship that is not really working for you and needs to end, what are the first three steps you need to take toward making this happen? What are three sources of caretaking you can put into place during this difficult time?

7. If you have a friend who consistently disappoints your expectations, have you ever discussed your feelings with them? If your friend is unwilling to change, can you release your expectations, or would it be healthier for you to cultivate friendships with people who share your expectations?

10

SILENCE IS DEADLY

The biggest communication problem is we do not listen to understand. We listen to reply.
—Stephen Covey

I know this seems romantic, but life isn't a movie. You have to discuss marriage, expectations, and what that entails.
—Arryana Luxe

In both chapter 5 and the previous chapter, we talked about how your expectations must be communicated. However, I want to do an even deeper dive on communication and how it can impact your relationships. Here's what I know:

**UNSPOKEN EXPECTATIONS ARE
RELATIONSHIP KILLERS.**

I'm going to focus on romantic relationships in this chapter, but if you're not in a romantic relationship, the information will still apply to whatever type of relationship you're dealing with (family, friends, etc.).

COMMUNICATE, OR ELSE

As we've all experienced, poor communication can have a devastating impact on relationships. In fact, it can damage relationships to the point where they are beyond salvaging. A study conducted by University College London, published in 2017, identified communication problems as the number-one reason for "the breakdown of marriages or live-in partnerships"; they were more prevalent than "growing apart," "arguments," and "unfaithfulness," which were all high on the list, but not at the top. The findings were so stark that researcher Dr. Kirsten Gravningen concluded that the frequency with which "communication and deterioration in the relationship quality are mentioned suggest[s] that there is a place for promoting better communication and conflict resolution skills in relationship counseling—including in the context of young people's sex and relationship education."

I'm all for that. I've already told you how attending counseling with my wife, Meagan, has helped us communicate with greater clarity and compassion, and to hear what the other really needs, not just our own interpretation based on our personal expectations.

One of the most valuable aspects of therapy is the lesson learned about how important it is to ensure that time and attention are set aside for regular communication. Not only is communication one of the two essential steps in setting your expectations, but without it, you may not be able to complete the other important step, which is determining if your expectations are realistic or not.

MAKE COMMUNICATION A PRACTICE
IN YOUR RELATIONSHIP.

I highly recommend that every couple do regular relationship checkups. You don't wait until your car breaks down to change the oil, right? You change it regularly. Relationships need tune-ups too. It's a good idea to do them as often as you need. Sometimes you'll need more frequent checkups, especially during a challenging time or when the two of you are trying to make a big decision.

The goal is to give and receive candid feedback. Start with basic questions like:

- Am I meeting your needs?
- Am I meeting your expectations?
- Do you feel like you're meeting mine?

The only condition is that both partners must be completely honest and willing to hear the other person's input without getting upset. If your significant other tells you that you're not exactly meeting their needs, or that there's an area that requires some work, that is not a criticism or a judgment. It's useful information you can use to improve your relationship. And if what your partner needs or expects is something you can't do, now is your chance to tell them, so they can reevaluate their expectations. Regular checkups will improve the overall quality of your relationship.

HOW BAKED CHICKEN TAUGHT ME MY
GREATEST LESSON ABOUT RELATIONSHIPS

Believe me, I have learned many of these truths the hard way, from my marriage with Meagan. Over the years I've had a variety of uncommunicated expectations. If baked chicken ever should have been called out in a couple's marriage vows, it should have been in ours.

When Meagan and I got married, I was excited. I was thinking: *Oh, man, this is great. I'm married now. I'm about to enjoy hot-from-the-oven, homecooked meals every day.*

And lo and behold, when we were newlyweds, Meagan started baking chicken.

Hallelujah, amen. Nothing like some good baked chicken.

Or at least that's what I thought the first few times she made chicken for me. Then, truthfully, there were some nights when I came home from work and expected maybe something a little different. But she had that baked chicken down. So I was all about gratitude for the chicken. I was thinking: *Hey, baby, bake that chicken. If that's all you got, go with it.*

I'm not kidding either. I was seriously grateful for that baked chicken. I thought marriage was great, and there was much contentment in our home. Then Meagan went to New York City for six months to star in a TV show called *Deception*. Now, this was no problem. I knew going into our marriage that Meagan is a talented, successful actress and that she'd occasionally have to be on location, sometimes for months at a time.

When she came back, I was very excited for some more of her baked chicken. I figured I'd give her a week to relax after she'd been working so hard, and then we'd resume our old routine. A week went by, I came home from work, and I didn't smell any baked chicken. All I caught a whiff of was cat litter.

Every night I checked the oven, I checked the microwave, I checked the refrigerator: nothing. No baked chicken. I began to feel upset, but I didn't tell her. I did that thing we've all been guilty of, where we are mad but we hold it in, where we don't express our expectations, or even our feelings. But she knew me well by this point.

She could sense that something was simmering below the surface of my cheerful facade.

"Hey, babe, everything all right?" she asked me.

"Yeah, I'm good, I'm good. We're good. I love you, baby. We're good."

But on the inside, I was like: *Yo, where's the baked chicken?*

I had created an unset expectation of her, and then I had done that thing it's dangerous to do but we all do it from time to time—I started to judge her decision not to cook for me. Now I was thinking: *Oh, clearly you don't love me. Clearly you don't care about being a great wife. If you did, you would know that I need this chicken.*

As we've already identified, in this pattern that can easily happen I allowed my unspoken expectations to warp my perspective, make me angry and resentful, and lead me to make a judgment and then an assumption—all without telling her any of this. But she could see that my disposition was off.

Finally, one day while we were watching the game at home, my true feelings burst forth: "Why aren't you making the chicken?"

This is how it happens. This is how what we suppress does not ever go away; it only festers until some little instigating incident makes us blurt out what's really going on.

At first, she was so surprised and just looked at me like: *Where did that come from?*

Now I had opened up the stopper, and it all had to come out:

"I don't understand why you don't care about me," I said.

She gave me a long look, and then she laid some truth on me:

"I could feel your expectation, and it took the joy out of it for me. I began to ask the question, *Will you still love me if I never make chicken again?*"

I sat there on the couch, dumbfounded, processing what she had said.

Thankfully, my lightbulb was not completely burnt out, and it slowly turned on:

Oh, got it. Love is supposed to be unconditional. What I'm doing is I'm making it conditional: you love me if you bake chicken. And I didn't even realize it. Or remember that if I love her and she loves me, love isn't supposed to be dependent on any condition. No, unconditional love is supposed to be unconditional.

Maybe that seems quick to have had such a big epiphany, but her words were so clear and heartfelt that I was able to see her point right away. In addition, as I dug further into my own thought process, I realized that I'd never set my expectations around cooking in our marriage because I never communicated with her about it. I'd never asked her how she felt about taking this on, if she agreed with my expectation or not, or if she had her own ideas on the subject. I made an assumption based on what I wanted, without even asking her what worked for her.

"Babe, you're right," I said. "I apologize. In our vows, it doesn't say I'll love you if you bake chicken. No, I'm going to love you no matter what. As a matter of fact, the last thing I want you to do is to think that my love for you is conditional. And if you choose not to cook, and if I choose not to cook, whatever, we'll figure it out. But I am no longer going to put an unspoken expectation on you and then treat you unfairly based on it."

By releasing the weight of that unspoken expectation, and by doing so together, our marriage went to another level. In that moment of truth, we set our expectations about cooking, together. Our decision was that we would take it day by day, but that neither of us would ever be obligated to cook unless we felt like it. And that's how we've handled it from that day to this.

As Meagan and I came to understand, these seemingly small conversations about daily expectations are not small at all—they are essential to setting expectations in order to form a stronger foundation for a relationship. Once we began to have them, both of us were actually able to give (and to receive) more.

When you have an unspoken expectation and you treat it like a spoken request, you are basically asking your partner to read your mind. Why would you wait, hope, and wish for your partner to do the impossible, when you could simply tell them what you're thinking, feeling, and expecting right now?

I've heard too many people say about their significant other, "If they love me, they should know what I like or what I want." Beware of this type of thinking. You are making an assumption about the deeper meaning of your partner's actions. Assumptions are dangerous, especially when they are based on incorrect information.

This could easily be the case in your relationship, especially if you've never had a direct conversation about whatever it is that's upsetting you. This kind of thinking can also turn into a mind game you play with your significant other. You mentally test them to see if they do the things you think they should do, and then when they don't, you dock them a point on your mental score card.

It is really difficult for someone to play a game well when they don't even know the game exists, let alone the rules.

LOVE HAS NOTHING TO DO WITH
SOMEONE'S ABILITY TO DECIPHER
ALL OF YOUR EXPECTATIONS.

Remember, relationships are a two-way street, so don't let anyone punish you for not meeting their expectations if they haven't communicated them to you. If you sense this is happening, ask the other person what they expected and why they felt let down. And then, once you are clear on their expectations, let them know if you can meet them or not.

Once you have communicated your expectations, your partner

may tell you they're not able to meet them. As we've discussed, it's up to you to handle your feelings around this disappointment, and then to figure out if there is a compromise that might work for both of you. After you've reached an agreement, then the expectation can be set—not a moment before.

What if you do communicate your expectations and your partner refuses to agree to meet them? How do you handle that? This can become a huge source of tension in relationships. I've seen couples try to control each other to get certain expectations met. This won't work.

If you're the one in the relationship who has an expectation that your significant other won't meet, you have to go back, reassess, and ask yourself:

- Why do I need this expectation met so badly?
- Can I meet it myself?
- What would happen if I let the expectation go?

If you're the one who can't agree to meet some of your significant other's expectations, you need to ask yourself:

- Why can't I meet this expectation? Am I being stubborn, resistant, or true to myself?
- How can I help my partner's expectation get met, even if I'm not the one who can meet it?
- If the relationship ends because of the unmet expectation, could I handle that?

All of this must be sorted out, especially if you have too many expectations that have been communicated but aren't being met. Unmet expectations can be a source of major pain and conflict. Talking through this issue can help you unpack why expectations aren't being met and work toward a potentially productive outcome. But resist the temptation to try to control or manipulate your partner to do what you want them to do.

CLEAN YOUR GLASSES

Your expectations of your significant other become the lenses through which you perceive them and their actions. If they are meeting or exceeding your expectations, then you perceive them as amazing. On the other hand, if they aren't meeting your expectations, you might be tempted to judge them—to look at them as less than loving, or to see them as less than amazing. As a result, your expectations can become a barometer by which you judge your overall happiness in your relationship. Just think of how unfair this is, especially if your perception is distorted and you haven't done your job and clearly communicated what you expect.

We all know how challenging communication can be in general. The stakes are even higher when you're attempting to express your relational expectations, which often requires a great deal of vulnerability. But not getting your expectations met can make you angry and upset, and your relationships, whether with your spouse, your parents, or your friends, often become complicated by these negative emotions. If you allow it to happen, these emotions can interfere with your judgment, smudging your lenses even more. Remember, everyone is their own person, with their own strengths and quirks, just like you. But your expectations can be preventing you from seeing others for who they really are, and for what they have to offer.

I'm going to challenge you to try something completely new in your relationships. For just one day—even just one hour—try removing all of your expectations from the equation. Set them aside. Don't think about them at all. And then look at your partner, friend, or family member through your new, crystal-clear lenses. See who they really are. Can you see now if they are or aren't who you thought they were (or were hoping they were)?

Whether they are or aren't who you thought they were, it's important to get a reality check on who they actually are. As we've discussed, expectations can skew our perspective. Real love is found in the truth of who someone is, not in the fantasy of who we hope for them to become.

WHAT LIES BENEATH

Secrets are destructive to relationships, and when they come to the surface, as they always seem to do, people are hurt and lives are ruined. That's the metaphor in the Robert Zemeckis supernatural thriller *What Lies Beneath*, a movie in which Michelle Pfeiffer and Harrison Ford play a married couple haunted by what's hidden beneath the surface of the lake near their house and the true story of how it got there.

In your relationship, what's lurking in the lake are all of your unset and unspoken expectations. And even more damaging are the resentments that simmer beneath the surface of your everyday interactions with your partner. When left unexamined and undiscussed, these resentments can fester and do real harm as you form judgments about your partner. But because none of this is out in the open, your partner has no way of knowing about your resentments, and therefore no way of making it right. Compounding the problem is that, even though it is your responsibility to speak your expectations out loud, if you are feeling hurt and angry you may be pulling away from your partner, rather than leaning into them and the communication that is necessary to heal what is hurting you.

Don't let any negative feelings remain hidden. Acknowledge them. Analyze them. Don't let them lurk in the shadows; bring them into the light of truth. Do your work to be aware of what you need, communicate it clearly, and do all of this candidly. You owe it not only to your partner but to yourself. It's the only sure way to move from hidden pain to visible happiness.

Don't be afraid to share how you really feel with your significant other. You have the opportunity to bring the two of you closer together. Think back to my baked-chicken story. Going into that conversation, I was projecting onto Meagan that if she didn't cook for me, it meant she didn't love me. But as soon as we talked through the situation, we got to the bottom of it. We both came out on the other side, feeling much more secure in our relationship—after a conversation about chicken! Think how much potential you and your partner have to really get to know each other when you express yourself.

If you find that you have been struggling to ask for what you need, that could reveal a self-worth problem. Because when you know who you are and what you're worth, you should feel less afraid to ask for what you want and need. First, you have to know that you're worthy enough to have your needs met, and that, even if your significant other gets upset because of your questioning, it's better to upset them than for you to remain silent and upset.

As long as you are actively communicating, you both have a chance to fix whatever isn't working. When you suffer alone in silence, no progress can happen. Start by clarifying your feelings:

- What judgments are you making of your significant other because they aren't meeting your unspoken expectations?
- What do you feel you need to communicate that would bring you and your partner closer?

EXPLAIN INSTEAD OF EXPECT

Change is possible, and relationships can and do improve and grow stronger, especially when both sides agree to work together toward setting shared expectations and releasing those expectations that can't be honored. Here's an example. Barack and Michelle Obama have had ups and downs in their relationship, just like everyone else. Early in their marriage, some of their problems were around unset expectations. Those led to different assumptions about how their union should function and what they both needed to be happy.

In opening up about all of this during an interview with Oprah Winfrey for a cover story in the November 2018 issue of *Elle*, Michelle Obama acknowledged that her marriage had taught her to "love differently." As Michelle said, "I've got two kids, and I'm trying to hold everything down while he's traveling back and forth from Washington or Springfield. He had this wonderful optimism about time. [Laughs] He thought there was way more of it than there really was. And he would fill it up constantly."

They clearly had different expectations about how much time they were both going to devote to the marriage and to being home with their young family. Obviously, Michelle did not demand that her husband give up his political ambitions. As she acknowledges in the interview, a career in politics doesn't offer much wiggle room—it's a 100 percent obligation, all of the time, especially to do it with as much passion and success as President Obama has done.

What she chose to do, out of love for her husband and commitment to her marriage, was to communicate all of this to him rather than letting the resentments pile up. They went to counseling together. During these sessions, she explored what happiness meant to her, and how to create more of it for herself within the parameters of her marriage. Also, Barack gave her some information that helped her understand his perspective and adjust her expectations and set them in a way that was more realistic—and therefore healthier—for both of them: "So, I had to share my vulnerability and also learn to love differently. It was an important part of my journey of becoming. Understanding how to become us."

This example is also a wonderful reminder of why it's never a good idea to make assumptions. If Michelle had assumed that, because it was easier for Barack to be away from her than it was for her to be away from him, he wasn't as committed to their marriage or their family as she was, or that he didn't love her, she would have been acting on an incorrect assumption. And she would have been missing out on the chance to get to know her husband better, and for both of them to become closer, by sharing their true selves.

YOU CONTROL ONLY YOURSELF (AND THE REMOTE)

You want a successful relationship? Then let go of any illusion you have of controlling the person you're in a relationship with. Too often, people assume they can get someone else to act or think the way they want. So many of us have brought unnecessary suffering upon ourselves by expecting the people in our lives to do things they never had any intention of doing—maybe even were incapable of doing. News flash:

> NONE OF US HAS THE ABILITY
> TO CONTROL ANYONE ELSE.

We often misunderstand, and don't even realize, that many of our relational expectations are unrealistic. It's one thing if you communicate your expectations to your partner and they agree to meet them. In that scenario, you're not controlling your partner—you requested something from them, they were able to honor your request, and they

did so. They had free will in the matter. That's how healthy relationships function.

You're asking for trouble, though, if you're manipulating your partner to do something by withholding something they want, or by pressuring them. It doesn't matter if you think what you want is justified,
or if you think your partner is wrong for not automatically doing it.
You are the one who's in the wrong—for resorting to coercion tactics
to try to control someone you profess to love. Instead, work on what
you can control, which is you.

> **THE SECRET TO SUCCESS IN RELATIONSHIPS IS
> TAKING YOUR FOCUS OFF THE OTHER PERSON AND
> PUTTING IT ON YOURSELF, WHERE YOU ACTUALLY
> HAVE CONTROL.**

Even if you're quite upset that your partner has said no to you,
it's important that you respect their decision. Since you don't have
the right to control other people, it's never okay to try to do so anyway. Believe me, I know it's tempting, but you're only asking for
trouble. Here's an eloquent discussion of the matter by the inspira-
tional speaker and author Esther Hicks: "It is easy to understand how
you would come to the conclusion that your path to feeling good is
through influencing or controlling the behavior of others. But as you
attempt to control them (through influence or coercion), you discover that not only can you not contain them . . . you simply cannot
get to where you want to be by controlling."

This is one of the hardest aspects of being in a successful relationship. I'm not saying your partner's behavior isn't important. It
is. However, you can be so conditioned to focusing on the behavior
you don't like in someone else that the thought of analyzing your
own behavior first is completely foreign. I've learned that anything

in your significant other that you're not liking is usually a reflection of the work you need to do on yourself. Great relationships stimulate the most growth. When you're being challenged by behavior you can't stand, look at it as an opportunity to grow and to become more loving, more compassionate, more considerate, and less judgmental. When you change yourself first, you will begin to see more of the changes you want to see in your partner begin to manifest.

TALKING IS ALL ABOUT LISTENING

When you are attempting to set your expectations, telling your partner about your needs is only the tip of the iceberg. It goes without saying that if you are only focused on your own needs, you are less likely to come out of the interaction with a positive solution for both of you. Just as important is listening to what your partner needs too.

There are several concrete tools you can draw on to become a better listener, according to the *Psychology Today* article "6 Surprising Ways to Communicate Better with Your Partner" by F. Diane Barth, LCSW. One of her tips is to "ask questions and don't assume that you know the answers."

Barth also offers a mini-lesson in a psychological technique called "active listening." Not only will this method of letting your partner know that you are *really* listening and hearing what they have to say help you feel more connected to each other, but it can also be a great way to diffuse tension during disagreements. This tool is incredibly valuable if you attempt to set an expectation with your partner and your partner pushes back, especially for a reason that you find unsupportive or unfair. Barth's suggestion is to be careful in the specifics of your communication, especially during moments of disagreement with your partner: "Interestingly, active listening can also involve interruptions for clarification or even disagreements. If you interrupt, be sure to ask permission. 'Sorry, can I ask you a question?' is a reasonable way to do it."

I know what you're thinking: this sounds good in theory, but in practice it can be very challenging to maintain control of your communication approach (and your emotions), if you strongly disagree with your partner's response. Again, that's why it's so helpful to come prepared with some of your thoughts written down. Focusing on that process, with the goal of communicating as effectively as possible, can help you avoid becoming too upset or emotional, which can work against the goal of successful communication.

In order to fine-tune your communication with your partner, ask yourself:

- When I ask my partner for something, do I let them consider my request and respond authentically, or am I guilty of only listening for the answer I want to hear?
- Was there a time when my partner didn't agree to an expectation I'd hoped to set and I could have pivoted to a more positive outcome by doing a better job of actively listening?
- Do I allow my partner to communicate their expectations to me?

Relationships are definitely an area of our lives where we're bombarded by external influences—from our families, from our friends, from pop culture. It's easy to take on outside expectations without even realizing it. The whole point of this book is learning to live free of them.

This means focusing on the real relationship you are actually having, with the person right in front of you, rather than the many different fantasies you might be projecting onto them (or they might be projecting onto you) about what your shared life *should* look like. Do your best to lean into the positive by turning your attention there at least some of the time. Ask yourself:

- What's the number-one way in which my relationship is unique and special?
- Have my partner and I ever communicated about why our relationship works?

The best way to strengthen and grow the relationship you are actually having with your partner is to listen to them (and let them listen to you). Listen to their hopes and dreams, yes, but also listen to what is working and what isn't. Be honest, be open, be an active listener, and you might be surprised at what you learn. Allowing your partner to be heard is one of the most thoughtful gifts you can give them, and when they feel heard by you, they will fall in love with you even more.

CHAPTER 10 Expectation Examinations

1. What currently unset expectation do you need to communicate to your spouse?
   i. What is your plan for asking to have your expectation met?
   ii. What will you do if your spouse can't meet your expectation?
2. Do you need to adjust the way you communicate with your spouse, or with others close to you, in order to be more responsive to the information they're giving you?

11

THERE'S NO CURE FOR SINGLENESS BECAUSE IT'S NOT A DISEASE

One of my favorite parts of being single is how I get to choose who I spend my time with, share my heart with, hang with, giggle with, call, dine across from.
—TRACEE ELLIS ROSS

If you don't act like you've been hit with the plague when you're alone on a Friday night, and just see it as a chance to have fun by yourself, it's not a bad day.
—TAYLOR SWIFT

Here's a public service announcement for anyone who's not in a relationship right now: there's nothing wrong with you.

We've focused on relationships in this section, and now I'd like to take time out to speak directly to those who are unattached. It's so difficult to avoid internalizing an incorrect perception, like the idea that there's some stigma attached to being single. Intellectually, we know it's unrealistic to expect to be married, in a long-term relationship, or even in love by a certain age. It's impossible to control whether or not this will happen. As with many expectations, if you've taken it on, even though you know better, it can interfere with your ability to be happy with your present life.

We need to start by shedding all of that old baggage. Relationship experts have said that the expectations created by online dating—too-hot-to-be-true photos, the ease of swiping left, "ghosting" with no consequences—are causing us to demand perfection, avoid commitment, and be less happy with our partners. As a result, unrealistic expectations and emotional breakups are more commonplace than ever before, and even dating successfully enough to enter into a relationship is harder than ever.

When I'm trying to help single men or women who are struggling with their lack of a relationship or with not being married, my first goal is to help them release the pressure of the ideas they've formed—or the pressure that's been put on them by their family or social circle. They believe they have somehow failed if they're not married by a certain age.

"You're thirty. So what?" I say. "Take that off of the table for a minute—your idea of what was supposed to happen by thirty—and live in the present. Find more freedom by enjoying the now, instead of becoming completely demoralized by an expectation that didn't get met—one that was based on a false set of standards anyhow."

I then ask them to look deeper—as I'm asking you now if you have a deep desire to be in a relationship or to be married—and answer this question: Why do you want it so much?

Don't rush to answer quickly. Stop and really think about how you learned about relationships, and what types of relationships were modeled for you growing up. Think about who in your life is in a relationship, or married, and how happy they really are. Think about how your friends talk about their relationship status, and if you agree with their attitudes or not.

We all have friends who just *had* to get married and rushed the process, only to end up miserable. Instead of taking the time to make sure they and their spouse had similar values and goals, they raced into an incompatible union. Think of how many marriages never would have happened if both partners had been totally honest with themselves and each other up front.

Of course, it's okay to think, *I'd like to be married.* However, the problems start when you turn this desire into an expectation that it must happen, especially within a certain time frame (which is beyond your control). And then you believe something is wrong with you if it doesn't happen. There's nothing wrong with you. If you find yourself obsessing over not being married, it's time to shift your focus. Instead of looking at being single as a detriment, I want to show you how it is actually a major benefit.

THE UPSIDE OF BEING SINGLE

For starters, being single allows you the opportunity to get to know yourself as much as possible. Glean all of the powerful personal revelations that you can. Ask yourself:

- What am I learning about myself during this period of time on my own?
- Who am I?
- Where do I want to go in my life?
- What do I like? What don't I like?
- What can I learn about myself from past relationships that didn't work?

Embrace these questions as an opportunity to know yourself better and to chart your course in life with greater self-knowledge and self-confidence.

Take the time to cultivate more gratitude for everything you have at this exact moment. Be grateful that you're not in an unhappy relationship. You have the space and time to work on yourself and to discover your own happiness. Make your life as vibrant and fulfilling as it can be in the present and you will be primed for a great relationship in the future, if you so choose.

Remember that as rewarding as relationships are, they also require energy and work to make them successful. Without that demand on you, there's more space in your life for self-care and self-reflection—and for the good kind of selfishness. You don't have to answer to anyone else when making decisions about how to spend your money (or not) and how to cultivate more and better ways to enjoy your own company.

These are only some of the benefits specified in the *Time* magazine article "9 Ways Being Single Can Improve Your Life." I think it's incredibly positive to remind yourself of the gifts of singlehood and to make sure that you're taking full advantage of them. The article also points out another, more subtle reward you might not have thought of, contributed by relationship expert and bestselling author Susan Winter: "Believe it or not, relationships are 'mentally' expensive. Intimacy and partnership takes up a lot of space in our heads. Even though much of this is happening unconsciously, there's simply a lesser capacity for individually focused thought."

Being in a relationship literally takes up more of our mental space, space we don't have available to devote to our own goals and interests. Of course, most of us in relationships are happy to make this sacrifice—we care about our partners and enjoy the benefits that come with a relationship. But Susan does raise a good point—as long as you have your full faculties completely to yourself, make good use of them.

When you are single, part of making the most of your life today is doing your best work to prepare yourself for the love that will arrive in your future. This means cultivating your happiness and your wholeness now by getting in touch with yourself about what you enjoy and taking advantage of your freedom to do more of that.

Develop yourself, pursue your passions, and expand your horizons. If there's a big life change you've been wanting to make—from going back to school to moving to a new city—now could be the perfect moment to go for it. Once you're in a relationship, some things will be much harder to do. Take a risk. Live outside the box. Whatever God is calling you to do, own it and do it. Our culture puts too much emphasis on the downside of being single, but when you live your life to the fullest, you will experience the upside of it.

Also, do more of what you love. Spend time with friends, take a class, start a business, or find a new hobby. Developing other interests and feeding other areas of your spirit and life will not only distract your focus from your current lack of romance but also increase the likelihood you'll be in the right place at the right time to receive the love you desire.

BE HERE (AND HAPPY) NOW

I've already established that no one is responsible for your happiness but you. If you think a relationship is the be-all and end-all and you're going to be happy when you're finally in one, that right there is an unrealistic expectation.

Take all of that attention you're putting on what you don't have and put it on what you do have: *you*. Make *yourself* happy now. If you are postponing or outsourcing your happiness and contentment to an unknown date in the future, you are setting yourself up for serious disappointment. The fantasy that marriage will instantly make you happy, that your spouse will be the answer to all of your problems and take away your loneliness, is one of the biggest myths in our culture. It's simply not true. Yes, companionship is awesome. And I'm a huge proponent of getting married *to the right person*. But even then, as we've discussed, you'll still be responsible for your own happiness.

Golden Globe Award–winning actress Teri Hatcher, who's been divorced twice, had this to say about being single to *People* magazine: "There is a difference between being lonely and being alone. I have been single for a very long time but there is nothing lonely about my life. I want to remove the stigma of that. . . . You are allowed to be proud of your life when you're not part of a couple."

If you are single, make the choice right now to work on improving your current happiness. Learn to take care of yourself, learn to attend to yourself and your needs, learn to find small moments of joy in your daily life. If you can pivot to live more joyfully when you're single, you are so much more likely to bring this happiness into your relationship when it does happen. Then a relationship is likely to only enhance what you already have. It won't be supplementing or subsidizing what you don't have.

LOVE AFFIRMATION FOR SINGLES

TO RECEIVE THE LOVE AVAILABLE
FOR YOU, YOU MUST BE OPEN.

Think about it this way—it is very hard to receive something if your fists are clenched. Try catching something with balled fists. It's not possible. In order to receive, you have to open your hands. In the context of your life, this is what I mean: if you are worried that you're not finding the right one and you're never going to find the right one; if you're doubting yourself; if you're wondering why you've been waiting so long, and why "the one" hasn't come into your life yet; if you're starting to lose hope that you're going to find love—and all of this is making you tense, that's the equivalent of closing your fists.

Just as you'd open your fists to catch a ball, open your heart to receive love. To do so, release any tension you may be feeling around when it will happen. You have your own love timetable. Some people receive romantic love early, and some receive it much later in life. Regardless of when it happens, I do truly believe that love is available to everyone.

However, if you are single and you want love, it's possible that you're working against your own desires. In order to receive love, instead of focusing on those who have it and wondering why you don't, or what's "wrong with you," focus on all of your positives. Tune in to the blessings you do have, not on what you don't have.

Yes, the timetable for your love story is out of your control. But here's one realistic expectation you can set. Repeat after me this love affirmation:

I receive what I believe.
I believe in me.
I believe in love.
I love myself.
I am the love I want to receive.
I release my anxiety.
I release my fear.
I release my doubt.
I open my hands,
I open my mind,
I open my heart.
I won't wait to love.

I love myself now,
I love my life now,
I love my love now.
I love God now.
I'm grateful for love now and the love I believe is on the way.
Amen.

Do not speak another negative word about your love life. Make this your daily affirmation. Commit it to memory. Repeat it as often as you can, especially when you get lonely. Desire love, but do not crave it. Craving is an energy that feeds your lower self. When you let your lower self lead, you will compromise who you really are, just to have someone in your life. Do not do it. It might feel good in the moment, but you will pay later. Truth be told, if you've compromised in the past, you might be paying for it right now.

Uproot any bitterness, anger, frustration, or fear from your spirit. Clear your heart. Become the love you want to receive. Instead of being distracted by what you don't have, shift your attention to what you do have: your health, your life, your job, your education, your church, your interests, your hobbies, your passions, your family, your friends, people who care for you. Instead of longing for love, become more loving. Live on the frequency of love. Get tuned in to it right now. I guarantee, when you do this, your positive energy will position you to receive love—not just romantic love but love of all kinds, coming to you from every direction.

NO SEX. NO PROBLEM.

As you may know, Meagan and I cowrote a book called *The Wait*, in which we talked about why we were celibate before we got married and the overall power of delayed gratification.

Now, I'm not anti-sex at all. Do I believe sex was created for marriage? I do. If that's not your choice, that's between you and God. If you choose to have sex before marriage, remember, it can alter your perspective in ways you're not always aware of. Before I was practicing The Wait, I experienced firsthand how much having sex with someone clouds your judgment. When you start dating someone new, preserving your good judgment should be one of your main objectives. You need to see this new person clearly. You want to discern their true intentions: Are they there for you, or are they there for the immediate physical gratification you can offer? Sometimes when you add sex into the mix, figuring this out can become impossible.

Celibacy can be especially challenging if you have not been in the habit of practicing it before. However, I highly recommend that you try it. There are many benefits. For example, you can take the wasted time and energy you were putting into chasing booty and use it to improve yourself in your body, mind, and spirit. You can put your focus on self-care—on healing, gaining perspective, and doing important self-assessments to cultivate wisdom, peace, and love. And you can reaffirm your faith that God is working on your behalf, so you don't have to frantically try to make anything happen. You'll become more confident, knowing blessings will arrive at the right time.

Making the decision to wait can be an incredibly empowering choice. However, maybe you believe your decision to wait is one reason why you're single. I understand. I have mostly heard from women who expressed their frustration about not being able to find a man who will wait with them. Many have told me that they've even flat out been left because they didn't put out. As I've told them, anyone who leaves you because you're waiting wasn't fit to be with you in the first place. If someone wants you to believe that sex is the admission price for love, ask yourself: *Is this the type of person I want to be with?* I hope not. Remember, you never have to compromise your beliefs for someone who doesn't share them. Your true love will appreciate and respect your values, even when it can be challenging and frustrating to do so.

SET EXPECTATIONS EARLY IN THE RELATIONSHIP

When you *do* start dating someone new, you should set expectations as early as is appropriate. This will help you learn more about the other person, as well as weed out anyone whose values and perspectives are totally different from yours. I'm not saying you should lay out your whole life plan while you're waiting to order on your first date. But even that early, you can be very clear about where your boundaries are.

For women, if you are interested in a man but do not want to have sex with him on the first date (or any date), be clear up front that you are looking forward to going out with him but will be paying your own way. Then there's no chance of him thinking: *Well, I paid for your meal, now I'm expecting to get something from you in return.*

If he's really insisting on treating you, or if you feel like being treated, come right out and set his expectations: "If you want to pay, thank you. I also need to set your expectation that I'm not sleeping with you. So, if that's a problem for you, let's go Dutch." The truth is, even in 2021, some men still think that wining and dining a woman implies a contract—that in return for dinner, she will be having sex with him at some point.

I know the thought of being so direct can make some people uncomfortable. However, it's hard to build a relationship if you can't even be honest about what your personal boundaries are. Or if you can't be honest with yourself about where it's going to lead you if you move forward with someone who you don't feel like you can talk to.

Again, if you're too fixated on checking that marriage box, you might compromise on your boundaries and values, in the hope of making this new person like you more. You would be much better off if you didn't waste time with someone who is in a different place than you, sexually, spiritually, or personally.

Ask yourself:

- Can I finally admit that when it didn't work out with that person who I thought was perfect for me, it actually saved me—by keeping me from living a false life?
- How can I make better choices going forward, for my heart, for myself, and for my life?
- What is one boundary I will not compromise on when I start dating someone new?

DATING 101: WHERE IS THIS GOING?

It can be hard to face the truth of your situation, especially if you don't like being single and you're afraid of losing the person you recently started dating. But I encourage you to be honest with yourself and to pay attention if you're dissatisfied for any reason. Never be afraid to ask: "Where is this going?" If your Uber driver was taking you somewhere other than where you wanted to go, you would ask them where they're headed. In much the same way, if you are not sure where your relationship is going, you must ask for feedback from the person you're dating.

So many people avoid doing this. They're afraid of receiving information they won't like that might force them to break up. Being in denial or avoiding the truth of a situation is never good. Sometimes people are afraid of putting too much "pressure" on the other person, or they fear that being too candid will "scare them away." But this kind of fear can prevent them from asking critical questions that could give them vital clarity on the other person's intentions or future plans.

If your partner is having their needs met, without needing to make any kind of a commitment or declaration of intent, they may turn out to be someone who could go on like this for a long time, maybe even years. But if you really want to be married, finally finding out that your partner has totally different ideas about the relationship and was never that serious can be devastating.

If you have been in this situation before, you know that the disappointment can break your heart and seemingly crush your hope. It can set you back emotionally, and it could even take you years to recover. That's why you can't afford to settle for less than you want or deserve. Be honest with yourself and the person in your life. Come right out and ask them:

- What are your intentions for this relationship?
- Are we on the same page? Do you feel the same way about me as I do about you?
- Do you want to get married eventually, to me or to anyone else?

This may sound harsh, but if the answers are not to your liking, stop dating that person right now. Maya Angelou famously said: "When someone shows you who they are, believe them the first time." Take a new dating partner at their word. If you don't like what they say, trust that they will never be the one you hoped they would become. I know this is hard to do, especially when you had great expectations for a person. However, resist the temptation to allow them to manipulate you into staying with them if they have already admitted they will never give you what you really want.

Now, even if the person you're dating answers all these questions to your liking and you think you've found the one, there's still no guarantee that marriage will happen. In fact, this is a common cause of tension in relationships. You want to get married and the person you're dating does too, but maybe not as soon as you would like. Is it worth sticking around, or should you cut the cord? I recommend using the same technique I advise for analyzing whether or not to leave a job: a cost-benefit analysis. Is the benefit of being in this relationship still greater than the cost?

If you are continuing to receive a greater emotional benefit from being with this person, then stay with them longer. Enjoy your relationship and see where it goes over time.

If being with this person is costing you more emotionally than the benefit you're gaining, it might be time to leave. How do you know if it's costing you? Assess your peace. Always be completely honest with yourself. If you're finding yourself more discontented than contented, more frustrated than happy, these are strong signs that the relationship is costing you. If you are holding out hope that the relationship will suddenly transform into a happy relationship later, even though you're not being fulfilled now, you're not being sustained now, or you're not being loved now, you could be making a devastating assumption. If you're not receiving enough out of it now, the odds are that you're not going to gain what you want from it later.

Try your best to honestly share your feelings with the person you're dating to see if your frustration or discontent can be addressed. If it can, wonderful. If it cannot, walk.

I understand that it can be scary to let go of a relationship, but I would argue that doing so can be your path to happiness in the one lifetime that you've got to live right now. And you owe it to yourself to make the best choice for your well-being.

RELEASE THE PAST

If you've been in a relationship that didn't work out and now you doubt yourself, that's understandable. We've all been there. But be encouraged—there's a solution. Another way to make the most of being single is to use this time to release your past. With no one else to take care of or be responsible for, you're in a great position to finally heal any open wounds, especially those suffered in a previous relationship gone wrong. In fact, letting go of old heartbreak is a powerful way to ensure that you're poised to embrace new love and commitment when it does appear in your life.

If you were in a relationship with someone you loved deeply and thought you were going to marry, but things didn't work out, I feel your pain. In my twenties, I was dating someone, fell head over heels for her, and was sure she was going to be my future wife. But things didn't work out. I cried big crocodile tears when it was over. I was heartbroken and defeated, and not sure I'd ever find love again (thankfully, I did).

If you're still feeling the sting from a breakup, this is the perfect moment to do the work to dig deeper, beneath the hurt, and examine any and all expectations you brought to that relationship.

If you truly believed you were going to marry this person, then you're grieving not only the loss of that relationship but also the loss of the future potential you assigned to that relationship. Ask yourself: *What is the best lesson I can take from this loss that will help me heal right now?*

Growth can only happen when we shine the light of honesty and humility into even the darkest corners of our lives. A critical component of being able to live free is to release your past pain. Living in the past will drive you crazy. No matter how much you examine the past or go over what happened, it will never change. It's so much better to live in the here and now.

Also, some things are not meant to be. You may have dated people who were not good for you and breaking up actually saved your life. They are the people who may have been leading you down a path that would have caused permanent emotional, physical, and/or mental damage.

Use this period of singlehood as a time to heal, to become whole, to receive revelations and realizations about your true self. And then use what you learn to make even better choices for your heart, for your health, and for your wholeness. Doing the work to heal from past hurts is one of the greatest gifts you can ever give to yourself.

CHAPTER 11 Expectation Examinations

1. Why do you want to be married, and how do you think it will improve your life?

2. Are there goals or interests you've put aside until you're married, like owning a house, traveling, or getting a pet? Is it possible that you could do these things on your own?

3. If there is someone in your life putting pressure on you to get married, do you need to have a conversation with them and tell them that their expectations are unrealistic and unhelpful?

4. What's one way you could be more present and enjoy your single life more today?

5. Is there a conversation you've been avoiding, with someone you're dating, a friend, or a family member, in which you have to make a boundary or need clear to them?

   i. How could you prepare yourself to have this conversation?

   ii. What's the worst that could happen if it doesn't go the way that you'd hoped?

Part IV

PROFESSIONAL EXPECTATIONS

12

THE PROCESS IS THE RESULT

How you climb a mountain is more important than
reaching the top.
—Yvon Chouinard

I want to practice to the point where it's almost
uncomfortable how fast you shoot, so that in the game
things kind of slow down.
—Steph Curry

In our professional lives, the rules are slightly different. Inherent in
having a job, whether you're the CEO or an assistant, is an exchange
of money for services. When it comes to setting your expectations in
your professional life, you have to be mindful of this fact. Every pay
period, in addition to whatever expectations you might have about
your own job performance, professional advancement, and career,

you're essentially agreeing to meet your employer's expectations in return for your paycheck.

We will discuss how to more effectively deal with this, but let's start at the source—*you*. What do you want to happen in your career? How is your current job helping or hindering you? Before I go any further, I need you to know that even if you don't like your current job, the way you choose to show up for work directly relates to whether or not you will succeed in achieving your dreams. What you will be you are now becoming. If you aren't meeting your employer's expectations and you think that somehow you'll be able to turn on excellence when you finally have a job you love, you're fooling yourself. Treat your current job like it's your ideal job, and you'll be living your dream job sooner than you think.

It's important to identify your professional expectations, independent of what your job expects of you, and whether they're realistic. If there's a huge gap between the two sets of expectations, you won't be happy. Maybe this disconnect is one of the reasons you're so frustrated right now. Consistently assessing if you're being realistic or not is critical to your long-term career success.

The answer to whether or not you're being realistic in your professional expectations can be boiled down to one word: *control*. Let's be honest, we're all control freaks—as I've said, I know I am. Any unrealistic professional expectations we have are likely due to our desire to control as much as we possibly can. I do believe that we are masters of our own destiny, but one of the keys to achieving this mastery is to have a firm grip on reality—you can only transcend your reality once you know what it is.

I've given advice to so many professionals who had illusions of grandeur about what they expected to achieve and by when. They were fixated on controlling what they didn't realize was out of their control. One of our greatest battles in life is recognizing and accepting that there's a great deal that's not in our power. We don't like that, but we need to understand and accept it.

For example, let's say your goal is to get promoted within a year. You set up a thoughtful plan; you analyze the best way to excel; you work overtime and volunteer for extra responsibilities; and you do everything possible to shine in front of your boss. Is the expectation of your promotion realistic or unrealistic? *Unrealistic.* Why? Your boss still controls that promotion, not you.

It's the same for how profitable or high-profile your business will become. I love to challenge business leaders by asking them, "No matter how hard you try, can any of you go make someone out there buy the product that you're selling?" Of course the answer is no. Obviously, this is frustrating. But instead of getting mad over what we can't control, we can focus on becoming a master of what we can.

YOU CONTROL THE PROCESS.

THINK OF THE PROCESS AS THE RESULT, AND YOU WILL BECOME MORE SUCCESSFUL.

Why is it so important to think of the process as the result? Because when we put so much energy, effort, and focus into a result we can't control, we aren't putting enough energy, effort, and focus into the process we do control. You may not be able to dictate exactly when you are promoted or when you receive a raise, but you can control arriving at work on time and doing the best job you can every day. You might not be able to control whether your customers buy your product, but you can control the quality of the product and the quality of your marketing and publicity. You can turn your career or business around right now if you embrace this revelation. Instead of stressing yourself out about what you can't control, unleash the power of what's in your control. The process is everything.

Here's the ironic part—the more you put into the process of your success the more you increase the probability that you will get the result you seek. This approach is actually a strategy to become more effective and productive every day. I live by this principle, especially when it comes to how I develop and produce my movies. From the studio that's financing the movie to the director who's helming it, to me, the producer—we all want the same thing: a great movie that is successful. But if we obsess over the box office numbers while, say, we are developing the script, our chances for success go down. Why? Because we're not putting enough thought and energy into developing a script that's good on its own merits. Commit to the process. It will take you everywhere you want to be.

THE PROCESS IS A SET OF DELIBERATE AND CONSISTENT ACTIONS TAKEN TO MAKE ANYTHING WITHIN YOUR CONTROL EXCEPTIONAL.

When making a movie, committing to the process means putting our focus on excellence—in the script, in the casting, in the production, direction, and so on. If we do this, no matter the result, we can all look at one another and feel good, because we know we did everything in our power to make the best film we could. There is no shortcut. Every successful outcome is the direct result of a successful process.

One of the wisest investors of all time, Warren Buffett, agrees. He summed up his professional approach in a 1989 letter to the shareholders of his company, Berkshire Hathaway, like this: "We enjoy the process far more than the proceeds." And that's saying a great deal from someone with a net worth of nearly $80 billion.

Inc. magazine elaborates in an article titled "Here's Why Warren Buffett Recommends Prioritizing the Process Not the Result":

"While outcomes, results, and final products are important goals to obtain . . . it may be more beneficial to devote your energy to the process instead. Warren Buffett expresses this very concept. This legend says you should focus on your methods, development, and actions instead of on your outcomes."

THE PATH TO MASTERY

Being process-oriented is also the surest way to achieve mastery. Take Terry Laughlin, a highly successful swim coach. He developed college and USA Swimming club teams that collectively earned twenty-four national championships through his unique method of swim instruction, Total Immersion. In Tim Ferriss's book *Tribe of Mentors*, Laughlin explains, "Life is not designed to hand us success or satisfaction, but rather to present us with challenges that make us grow. Mastery is the mysterious process by which those challenges become progressively easier and more satisfying through practice."

The good news is that, as Terry points out, challenges get easier. The more you apply yourself the more you will build successful momentum, especially if you remain focused and disciplined. It still takes work. However, when you devote yourself to the process, you'll inevitably improve in the areas of your focus. And the feeling of doing well will be its own positive result, with powerful personal and professional rewards.

Mastery is a topic I became well versed in when I was researching and writing my last book, *The Truth About Men*, which taught men and women how to gain control over the destructive force of their lust (not only for sex but also for money and power) by learning to master themselves. I was very candid about the fact that it's not always a comfortable or fun method—it can be tempting to take the easy route and just go with what feels good in the moment. But the

cost of unchecked lust is so great that it has brought many powerful men (and women) to ruin in both their professional and personal
lives. And the rewards of pursuing anything in life—whether it's a
romantic partner or a job promotion—with greater self-control and
personal honor are priceless.

My advice from *The Truth About Men* on the benefits of mastery in
the professional realm definitely apply here. As I made clear in that
book, how we do what we do overrides everything else. It may be
tempting to seek shortcuts, but instead, we must commit to the process and value integrity over the speed of our advancement. Masters
have no time line; their focus is on achieving true success, no matter
how long it takes.

Look at your current process, and ask yourself:

- What's a skill I could master that would help me improve my
  performance on the job?
- What tools are available to help me gain mastery (an online class,
  a mentor, a book, a networking organization, a one-on-one with
  my boss to learn where I could improve)?
- Has there been a time when I lowered my integrity in my lust for
  professional success? If so, how will I do better in the future?

MY EXPECTATION BREAKDOWN

I'm not telling you anything that I haven't learned first myself.

SOME OF LIFE'S LOWEST MOMENTS BECOME
OUR GREATEST TEACHERS.

It was 2010, and I was a vice president of production for Sony Pictures Entertainment. The previous year I'd overseen the production

of the remake of the classic movie *The Karate Kid*, starring Jaden Smith and Jackie Chan.

This had been a huge undertaking—not only because of the level of the stars involved, and their commitment to quality in everything they do, but also because we filmed in Beijing, China. At that time, an American movie hadn't been shot there since *The Last Emperor*, in 1986. During the production, I'd worked harder than I ever had before; I traveled to China nine times in nine months. When I wasn't there in person, there were many nights when I'd be in my office in Los Angeles at 1 A.M. and 2 A.M., so I could communicate with producers when they were on set. (There's a fifteen-hour time difference between Beijing and Los Angeles.)

We had made the movie for around $40 million, and its opening weekend in North America it grossed $56 million; it went on to earn $359 million worldwide. It was a huge hit and became very profitable for the studio. So of course I thought there was nothing wrong with expecting that I was going to get promoted. After all, I had worked so hard on the project, and it had done so well.

However, that's not what happened. In fact, my bosses at the time told me the exact opposite: they wished they could promote me, but they couldn't. There were already too many senior executives. Instead of being in charge of my own movies, I would need to go back to supporting other executives on their movies. I couldn't believe it; this was a huge blow, and I was completely devastated. Back then I couldn't see that, although I'd had plenty of big expectations, they'd all been unset—they'd been both unrealistic and unspoken.

This is why there's such a huge distinction between setting your expectations and letting your unset expectations tornado through your life, causing disappointment and hurt. This is why all expectations must be set.

For a few months, I was so depressed that it was hard to get out of bed when I woke up in the morning. It was hard to exercise. It was hard to pray. It was hard to make myself go into the office and engage with my colleagues. And while I'd always been a person with a bunch of goals that I was really passionate about achieving, and a ton of energy to move them all forward, none of that was in play. It had all screeched to a halt. Out of my anger about having my expectations disappointed, I'd given up on my life and myself.

That was a very dark time. It wasn't even about the promotion; it was about my own self-worth and the value I had assigned to a promotion. I associated my self-worth so closely with a promotion that, when that didn't happen, it felt like I didn't receive what I was worth. And as a result, I felt worthless.

Now, looking back, I realize how overblown my expectations were, but at the time this was really how I felt. I said to myself, *I'm going to do away with expectations altogether.* But that created another problem: without any expectations, I had no motivation. I had no forward movement toward goals, or toward anything else. I had no hope. I was beyond stagnant. I would ask myself: *Why am I working so hard? Why am I fighting so hard?* I was not functioning at all. Before long, I realized that I needed some expectations, not just to thrive but, honestly, to survive. That's why all of us need expectations.

This challenging moment in my career actually ended up being a blessing in disguise. It forced me to really assess my life, determine who I was, and think seriously about where I wanted to go. I had to dig deeper inside myself to discover something that I otherwise might never have uncovered: *I am created to create. To be successful I have to create, not just manage the creation of others.*

This one revelation has powered my life and career from that day to this. Now, there is nothing wrong with managing the creation of others. I'm just saying this was my own personal epiphany, and it eventually caused me to make some major life decisions, like starting my own company, which helped me feel excited about my future again. It was a journey that took time, but one that built momentum as my feelings of potential and positivity returned.

I did allow my experience with *The Karate Kid* to take my hope for a time. I was so focused on the results, on getting exactly what I wanted out of that movie, without realizing that the process was the true result. When my expectations went unmet, I let my bosses and my disappointment lessen my sense of self-worth—at least for a little while.

BREAK YOUR ADDICTION TO RESULTS

I'm sure all of this makes good, logical sense. The problem is that we're not just trying to adopt a new way of thinking and behaving. We're also counteracting a lifetime of messaging that has taught us to be results-oriented. As a culture, we are so addicted to results, and not just in our careers. We want to look a certain way. We want to have a certain car and live in a certain house. We want to marry a certain person. **We want the result.**

That's what marketing is all about—it sells us the promise of results all day long. We scroll on our phone and it's all we see: take this new supplement to be skinnier, wear these new jeans to be hipper, listen to this new song to be cooler. The focus is on the outcome, which almost never materializes as easily as advertised.

WE HAVE TO BREAK OUR ADDICTION TO RESULTS.

Now, I know this may sound absolutely crazy, but it's true. I'm not saying results don't matter—of course they do. There are many results I want to achieve at any given moment in my life. What I'm saying is that our addiction to results has damaged our ability to actually achieve the results we seek. We have to become addicted to committing to our process instead. Do so, and it will develop skills in you that you may not even recognize until years later. And those skills will help you along your way.

Let's look at my story about working on *The Karate Kid* and how my unrealistic expectations about earning a promotion caused me to lose hope. A little time and greater perspective have shown a whole new light on that story for me. In actuality, as much as I wanted and expected the promotion, I wasn't working hard on that movie for the promotion (the results); I really was working for love of the work itself (the process).

Yes, I was giving a lot of myself to making the movie, and the hours were crazy. But I wasn't mad that I was in the office at one o'clock in the morning. I was committed to the project and willing to do whatever it took to make it successful. I was committed to excellence and to doing my best at the work that was in front of me. There was no question that I was going to give it my all, twenty-four hours a day. So that was my process, and because that's where my focus was—intent without expectation—I was enjoying the work.

And then, yes, I was temporarily sidetracked when I wasn't promoted. But it didn't take me all that long to get back on my feet and to use all of those skills I had mastered during the making of that film to do bigger and better things in my career. When I eventually set out on my own, forming my production company, Franklin Entertainment, I began to realize as I started developing and producing my own movies that my experience making *Karate Kid* actually prepared me to run my company successfully, because now I knew what to do. So my commitment to being process-oriented set me up for greater future results and overall success.

PERFECT YOUR PROCESS

While results can be elusive at times, there are a number of positive adjustments you can make to your process right now, no matter where you are in your career. One of the tweaks I recommend is analyzing and learning from your mistakes, as well as those made by others. All successful entrepreneurs and business leaders use this approach. Inevitably, we stumble and misjudge the situation sometimes. But anyone who's reached the top of their field has managed to find the lessons in their past blunders and used them to make better decisions moving forward. Even better, they often can distill their wisdom into valuable advice.

There's no substitute for doing your own research, analysis, and critical thinking, as the Nashville-based entrepreneur Brigette Edwards told *Inc.* magazine: "I made a bad purchase because I didn't perform my own due diligence. I took the easy route and didn't completely commit myself and my time. I learned you can't commit halfway and succeed."

Of course, it's easy to point to what someone else did wrong and extract a nugget of knowledge or insight. The trick is to approach your own process the same way. Mistakes are inevitable—we all make them (even Mr. Perfect)—so rather than beating yourself up, look at mistakes as a valuable part of your process. Mistakes can give you so much power—they work for your good, not against your good. Business guru Ray Dalio calls mistakes "the body of evidence," there and ready to be evaluated. Even negatives can become positives when you learn how to use them to strengthen your process. In order to learn from your errors, ask yourself:

- What are the top three mistakes I've made at my current job?
- What can I take from each of these mistakes?

- How can I apply these lessons so as to avoid making these mistakes again?

Growing from your past mistakes is just one way to enhance your process. Productivity is another. When are you the most productive? For example, Jud Bowman, the founder and CEO of Sift Media, made this contribution to *Inc.* magazine's survey of some of the top CEOs for its Inc. 5000 list, asking them for the rituals and tips that helped them the most: "A few years ago, I noticed that on long flights, I got an amazing amount of work done. . . . So now I try to replicate this 'airplane mode' during the day when I want to focus and get a lot of work done."

As you'll notice, this is a very small shift, but one that has obviously had huge results for Jud. The most important feature of this example is that Jud was self-aware enough to know when his process worked best, and then to re-create those circumstances elsewhere in his life. Too often we're just running all the time, busy to the max, trying to keep up with a million deadlines and obligations. We forget that we need to focus—to limit distractions and bring our best to each task or project. It makes a difference for even high achievers like Jud. After learning this lesson, he wouldn't make the mistake of working in a distracting environment again.

Your process can and should be tailored to your particular strengths and goals: how you set out to improve yourself, how you do your job, how hard and long you work in any given week; or, if you're a leader, how you run your company and interact with your employees. Although your process will be made up of many different goals and tasks, it should be something you can measure: how many more hours you decide to put into working on something to gain greater mastery; how many books you read to gain a new skill; or how many people you network with during the week to advance your career.

Anything that is going to be a part of your process must be something that you can control, by changing your behavior or seeking out new information or expertise. Your process for success should be reviewed and tweaked as you grow and improve. The most important aspect of your process—other than sticking to it—is approaching it with flexibility. A static process will not be nearly as powerful as one that you are constantly adjusting, based on your progress and results, as well as any new responsibilities, skills, or assets you may gain. A process should grow with you and your career.

Ask yourself:

- Is there a time of day, or a certain location, that inspires me to be focused and productive?
- What are the top three distractors that get in the way of my professional process? Is there a way I could remove them completely, or at least minimize them?
- How could I be more effective as a member of my team, or more generally, at work?
- If I could convince my boss to make one improvement in our work process, what would it be and why? How could I most successfully communicate this suggestion?

TEAMWORK MAKES THE DREAM WORK

Even though you may be keeping your process side of the street clean, you may be looking around your workplace in frustration at how disorganized and faulty other people's processes are. Well, as we've already determined, you can't control other people's behavior, which means you definitely can't control their processes. But since most jobs do involve working with others, it can be helpful to make a strategy for trying to improve the overall process of any team you are a part of.

For example, let's examine one of the arguably greatest teams of all time, the Chicago Bulls of the 1990s, and particularly the 1997–1998 basketball season, when they sought their sixth league championship in eight years, as featured in the 2020 docuseries *The Last Dance.* While the series understandably highlights the tensions among the team's players, and between players and management, which were dramatic and made for great TV, it took the whole team to win the championship that year.

The team had a slew of stellar athletes, including Scottie Pippin and Dennis Rodman, but the star was Michael Jordan, who was the first to admit he had a very high expectation of himself on the court. "My mentality was to go out and win, at any cost."

He was focused on being his best, and he expected the same of his teammates. But he didn't ask anything of them that he wasn't willing to deliver himself. Michael was notorious for being the first to arrive at practice and the last to leave. As celebrated as he became, he never stopped putting in the hard work, or remembering back to the times he had failed as a way to spur himself on to work harder and do better. He famously said, "I've missed more than nine thousand shots in my career. I've lost almost three hundred games. Twenty-six times I've been trusted to take the game-winning shot and missed. I've failed over and over and over again in my life. And that is why I succeed."

Michael has spent a great deal of time refining his process, both as an athlete and a businessman, and so he is able to make clear assessments—like this one—of what made him excel as an individual player. And yet, as much as he might have famously butted heads with other players on his team, he has always been quick to celebrate that team as well. He himself pointed out that, while he'd achieved a great deal throughout his career, it wasn't until the right team fell into place around him that the Bulls reached the pinnacle of their playing and winning. As he has observed: "If you think and achieve as a team, the individual accolades will take care of themselves. Talent wins games, but teamwork and intelligence win championships."

Now, you might think that the successes of Michael Jordan—one of the most gifted and driven athletes in the history of sports—have little to do with your own life. Maybe you're just trying to get along in the nine-to-five. But he remains a powerful example, because he shows how one person's insistence on excellence—and willingness to work hard to get there—can light a fire under an entire group of people. Learning to harness the power of your coworkers and their individual strengths can be a great way to achieve even more, and to find a rewarding sense of community.

If you apply Michael's tried-and-true methods to your own job, will you find success? I believe you will. When you decide, as a committee of one, that you are going to commit to the process and lead by example, you can compel even the most resistant person on your team to step up their game. Here's what Michael had to say about his own process for being prepared: "The minute you get away from fundamentals—whether it's proper technique, work ethic, or mental preparation—the bottom can fall out of your game, your schoolwork, your job, whatever you're doing."

That's why Michael put in the extra time at practice, was relentless in drilling his shots, and didn't shy away from acknowledging and analyzing his mistakes on the court—these were all means of strengthening his fundamentals. And while his interactions with his teammates were always blunt, they never doubted his passion for their shared goal—playing their best and winning—and they always knew that he came as prepared as possible each and every day.

Think about ways you could improve your own fundamentals at your job. What would happen if you went in to work an hour earlier every day and used that time to take on the tasks that always seem to fall to the bottom of the to-do list, or to develop a new skill or strength that would benefit not only you but also the members of your team?

What if you sought feedback from others about areas where your work could support their work better, or where you could more efficiently collaborate, to improve workflow and productivity? Again, it's not just about blindly doing more, or piling more obligations on top of yourself. Quite the opposite—our approach is all about taking on less, more mindfully, to do it better and achieve more freedom. Ask yourself:

- Is there a task or requirement I avoid at work because it's not my favorite, or it makes me feel out of my depth? What if I leaned in and focused my attention there instead?
- Is there someone I could collaborate with at the office in order to make up for areas where I'm not as strong, or to launch a new initiative that I can't handle alone?

THE RICHER THE SOIL THE BETTER THE GROWTH

The process is the soil. The result is the plant. If you want to improve your chances of something great growing—of achieving the best possible result—then you enrich the soil as much as you can. You remember that, if you don't water that soil and provide the right amount of sunlight, the chances that you are going to grow what you want are very slim. But when you're attentive to the soil and make sure what you're growing has everything it needs, including water, sunlight, and plant food, the chances that you are going to grow what you want are extremely high. Life operates the same way. If you aren't getting the professional results you want, your soil is too dry.

So do an assessment: What's feeding your soil? Vigorously evaluate all of your processes. Ask yourself:

- What are my expectations for where I will be in my career in four months? In four years?

- What are my expectations for where I will end up in my career?
- What are my expectations for how much I should earn for the work I do?
- What are my top three goals in life right now?

Take one goal at a time and write down the key steps in the process by which you plan to achieve it. Are they all within your power to complete? To answer this question, you may need to seek out a mentor, or have an informational interview with someone who currently holds the position you'd like to achieve. Ask specific questions about special degrees, training, or skill sets that were necessary to get to where they are.

If you're lacking in any of these areas, can you make up for this deficit by going back to school or expanding your duties in your current job in order to gain these skills? If not, do you need to adjust your process, or maybe even change your goals? Keep doing this type of analysis, until you have settled on a realistic expectation for where you want to be.

Also, when you get real about your process, you should start to gain a more comprehensive understanding of your strengths and weaknesses and how you fit into your larger team. Getting the objectivity necessary to realize and accept this, and then to implement positive change in the right direction, can be challenging. But it's crucial to do so, as Ray Dalio makes clear in his book *Principles*. One of those principles, "Embrace Reality and Deal with It," was an important step in building up to the kind of next-level success he achieved at his hedge fund, Bridgewater Associates. Dalio advises: "Asking others who are strong in areas where you are weak to help you is a great skill that you should develop no matter what, as it will help you develop guardrails that will prevent you from doing what you shouldn't be doing. All successful people are good at this."

As Ray goes on to point out, it can be extremely difficult to be objective about ourselves and what we are and aren't good at, so you may have to start by asking someone you can trust for their input. What you're looking for is an honest assessment of where you're at, how effectively you're working and collaborating with others, and what you could be doing better. This type of feedback can be extremely useful, so don't fear it. Seek it out.

Instead of looking only for your faults, you'll actually be looking for ways to improve yourself, and then to use those improvements as fuel for your next win.

CHAPTER 12 Expectation Examinations

1. What are your top five professional expectations? Once you have listed them, organize them in order of significance or weight, from most to least important.

2. Think about your career. How much of your dissatisfaction has more to do with where you were expecting you would be at this point than with the progress you've actually made?

3. What are the top three items in your daily professional process that could use an upgrade? (Some examples might be going to bed earlier, eating better, or reading more about your field.)

4. Are there any areas of your professional life where you've gotten what you expected but you're not satisfied? Is it possible that you're just falling back on the common definitions of success or fulfillment and that, if you dig deeper, you might find something more personal that you're craving—like more time, more freedom, more meaning?

13

FIX YOUR GOALS

If you want to be happy, set a goal that commands your thoughts, liberates your energy, and inspires your hope.
—ANDREW CARNEGIE

Success is the progressive realization of a worthy goal or ideal.
—EARL NIGHTINGALE

Pilots learn a lesson about flying that also applies to life. It's called the one-in-sixty rule: if you are off by just one degree in your flight coordinates, after traveling sixty miles you'll be one mile off course. This may not seem like a big deal, but consider the following, as calculated by programmer and entrepreneur Antone Roundy:

- If you were traveling from San Francisco to Los Angeles, you'd be off by six miles.

- Go from San Francisco to Washington, DC, and you'd end up on the other side of Baltimore, 42.6 miles away.
- Take a rocket to the moon, and you'd be 4,169 miles off.
- Heading toward the sun, you'd miss by more than 1.6 million miles.
- Traveling to the nearest star, you'd be off course by more than 441 billion miles.

Do you see how being off even one degree can make a tremendous difference?

Now let's apply that idea to your goals. When you take aim at your goals, the very trajectory of your life could be thrown entirely off course if you are off in setting the goals you're pursuing. Goals won't work if they're based on unset expectations.

> **IF YOU HAVE TOO MANY UNSET EXPECTATIONS,**
> **YOU WILL CREATE FAKE GOALS—GOALS THAT**
> **LOOK GOOD BUT AREN'T.**

GET REAL ABOUT YOUR GOALS

I remember that, back in my early twenties, I would go with my great-aunts down to Santee Alley in downtown Los Angeles. Known as "The Alley," it's the place in LA to buy designer fashion for cheap, and at the time it was also where you could find knockoff watches. I was a college student and didn't have the means to buy the Rolex of my dreams, so I went to The Alley and got a fake one for less than $100. Now, when I wore it, it looked real to the outside observer, who would have seen that it wasn't if they were to look more closely. This is exactly how fake goals operate: they look legitimate, but if you examine them more closely, you see that they aren't real. They've been created from false (unset) expectations.

When something is expected of you, you create a goal to meet it. When you're expecting something, you create a goal to make it happen. Expectations create goals, and goals create expectations. It's important to properly align your goals with your expectations. It is a key component when it comes to living a fulfilled life.

How do you know if you're chasing fake goals? You must analyze your expectations that are connected to your goals. To do so, pay attention to how your goals make you feel. I believe goals connected to set expectations will energize us and keep us motivated, even during downtimes. However, if your goals are making you feel worse instead of better, there's a problem. Looking back, I've realized that at various times in my life my own unrealistic expectations informed how I established and created fake goals. Whenever I had fake goals, even though they were respectable on their own merits, I often felt dissatisfied.

For example, when my book *The Truth About Men*, my fourth publication, was released in February 2019, I had lofty expectations, which I translated into goals. I wanted it to be my biggest book and to hit the *New York Times* bestseller list, so I made a vow to myself: *I'm going to make this book a success. I've got to go out there and do everything it takes.*

My campaign got off to a promising start, and the number of people who preordered the book before the sale date was solid. I was grateful for each and every person who believed in me and my message enough to support the book, from the publisher to the book buyers, and I hoped they would be moved by my words.

I did close to a hundred interviews, on radio and TV and for digital and print outlets—anywhere they would have me, big or small. For six months, I drove myself relentlessly. In April of that same year, a film I'd produced, *Breakthrough*, was being released. I went right from the book promotion into the film launch, and at some events I was promoting both at once. My feeling was: *Go, go, GO! I'm Mr. Perfect, I can't stop now. I've got to have a hit!*

This mentality was taking its toll, but I didn't realize how much. When I started doing press for my film, the difference in how I looked between January and April was striking. You could see the evidence of absolute fatigue on my puffy face. I was weary from working myself to the bone, in the belief that if I didn't, I would never achieve my goals.

The strain didn't go unnoticed. At the *Breakthrough* premiere in LA, I was approached by my close friend and mentor Elizabeth Cantillon. She pulled me aside and, after congratulating me on the film, expressed her deep concern. "Oh, DeVon, you need to slow down," she said. "You're working too hard. I can see it all over your face."

Even with the deep respect and admiration I have for Elizabeth, and even as weary as I was undeniably feeling at the time, I didn't really register the significance of her words. I was too consumed by the sales goals I had set for myself. As has always been my nature, I was going to meet them, no matter what. So I continued to push, until we were far enough past the publication date that there was really nothing more for me to do to promote the book.

Ultimately the book sold well, but it wasn't my biggest, and it didn't hit the *New York Times* bestseller list. I had failed to reach my goal. The result didn't match my expectations—or my Herculean efforts—and I felt like a failure.

Ever been there before? Well, if you are anything like me, it's hard to accept this feeling. I'd believed that if I worked hard, I'd get the result I wanted. I'm still a proponent of rigorous work, but I've learned the hard way that work in and of itself isn't a guarantee of anything except exhaustion. I see so many people working hard and wearing themselves out instead of working smart. Working smart is creating goals from set expectations and using the appropriate amount of labor to attempt to make them come to fruition.

With all the book and film promotion I'd been doing, I'd uncon-sciously slipped back into my old role of Mr. Perfect—who equated self-worth with perfectly achieved results. But in this case, my re-sults weren't "perfect." They weren't even as good as I'd hoped. It got dark there for a time. My expectations were unrealistic—impossible, really—and had led me to set fake goals. Now all I could see was that I hadn't hit them. I started talking to myself in a negative way:

Man, DeVon, you don't have what it takes.
You're not as successful as you think you are.
Your voice isn't as prominent as you wish it would be.
You're not as influential as you would like to be. Dude, you're not that guy.

Once I returned home from being on the road, promoting, for months, I was able to have some much-needed downtime. It was only then that I could finally feel the drain of the exhaustion that Elizabeth had spoken to me about. I took time to rest, be still, and hear from God. In that stillness of prayer, meditation, and good ole soul-searching, I had a major revelation: *I'm tired. I can't keep running like this. Something has to change. I need some help.*

I started to understand the need to set realistic expectations for myself—the first kernel of what would become this book. Viewing my goals—not just for my book's performance but also for myself—through the lens of this new understanding, I could see that they were fake, and that they'd been fake ever since I'd begun running that secret "Mr. Perfect" software.

What made my goals for my book fake? They were based on some-thing that was out of my control—the number of books that were sold. We'll talk more about what we can control, and what we can't, in later chapters. But here I can definitely say that, because how many people bought my book was something I *couldn't* control, it was unrealistic to aim at a certain number as a goal. Now, there's nothing wrong with hoping that a book reaches a certain level of success, but my real goal should have been related to my process, not obsessing over my result. So I know firsthand how not getting the result we want can give us a crisis of confidence in what we're doing, and in ourselves, if we let it.

During this downtime, I knew I had to make some major changes in my life. Once I become clear on what needs an upgrade, I'm the type of person who goes after it immediately. I started by releasing unrealistic expectations (like perfectionism) and focusing instead on appreciating who I am and finding more gratitude in my life. I rewrote a toxic belief I'd long held: *I have to do in order to be.* I replaced it with a healthier belief: *I know I'm not perfect, and I don't even want this ideal I've set for myself.* I started working on, and am still working on, learning to be okay with me, not the striving me but the me God created. And I reached out for concrete help—I started working with a life coach and a therapist.

My point of view now is completely different. I choose to focus on all the copies of my book that did sell, not on those that didn't. Each and every book sold represented a person whose life I helped to improve. I hear from readers constantly about that book and its positive impact on their lives. I now choose to focus on my gratitude for that book. It furthered my career as an author by enabling the book you're reading now, which I know has the power to transform your life. It's another book, by the same author, with sales figures accruing once again, but when I look at it without the skewed perspective created by fake goals, I have a totally different understanding of it, and a totally different level of personal contentment from publishing it.

Are you feeling dissatisfied? This is a good sign that either you have fake goals or you're losing faith that your goals will come to pass. Real goals should motivate you, not only to achieve the goal but also to bring the necessary discipline to seeing it through. When thinking about your goals doesn't make you feel good, you have fake goals.

I know I'm not alone in this. It's why people often describe an empty feeling they have after accomplishing a goal they've been working toward for years. This happened to me as a young studio executive. One of my other obsessions had been becoming a vice president of production by age thirty, but that didn't happen. When I eventually did get the title and promotion, my rush of excitement lasted only a few days and was followed by the thought: *This is it?*

I had made the mistake of expecting that the title would give me a feeling of significance and accomplishment. I was wrong. It was a fake goal. I'd based it on an unrealistic expectation: *Once I receive the promotion to vice president, I'll feel more important, and I'll feel like I am somebody.*

What I eventually came to realize was that no title was going to satisfy me. I had to find fulfillment within myself first, rather than looking for it from anything or anyone outside of me.

In order to set real goals, I've also begun taking the time to delve deeper into the "why" of what I'm trying to achieve—to look beyond the surface accomplishments of box office numbers and book sales to think about what's motivating me to create these films and books in the first place. I've discovered that one of my real and main goals in life—the one that truly drives me—is inspiring and uplifting others in as many ways as I can. This clarity has helped me set all of my expectations accordingly. And I make sure my process and my goals align in the service of these expectations on a daily basis. As a result, I'm much more content—not just with my work life but with its outcomes, even when they sometimes surprise me.

So, as with expectations, you must analyze your goals. Make sure they're really of your choosing and release any that aren't—along with any goals that might be unrealistic, no matter how hard you work. Let's start by letting go of fake goals. Ask yourself:

- Was there a time when I achieved what I thought was an important goal, only to feel disappointed and empty?
- Looking back, can I see now that I was pursuing a fake goal?
- By contrast, what are some goals I've achieved that have proven to be in keeping with my greater purpose in life? Can I cultivate more of those types of goals?

SETTING THE GPS SYSTEM OF YOUR LIFE

There are many sources of fake goals, yet some of the most common are the expectations your family or friends put on you. You've accepted them, and as a result, you have chosen to pursue a certain life path, even though it's not really what you're called to do. You may have accepted these expectations to make your parents happy, or to gain acceptance or praise from your friends.

If you have unquestioningly accepted someone else's expectation of who you're supposed to be, and then chosen the life you feel you're supposed to live that goes with that expectation, it's highly likely you are setting a destination for your life that's far different from the one you were created for. It's like using the GPS app Waze to get somewhere. If you enter the wrong address, Waze will direct you to whatever location you've put in. Life is the same way. It might send you to where others want you to go, but is that where *you* really want to go? It's up to you to identify if this has happened (or is happening) in your own life, and to course-correct as soon as possible.

Here are some questions to ask yourself to help you begin the course-correcting process:

- Am I pursuing this goal for myself, or do I feel like I have to go after it in order to prove to my family (or someone else) that I am successful?
- If I do "make it" and achieve this goal, whose dream am I living in service of?
- What do I believe the achievement of this goal will bring me?
- If there were no perceived negative consequences, what would I really want to do?

If you answer these questions honestly, you will be taking a powerful step toward realigning your life on the correct course and getting on track to where you are supposed to go: living the life of your own choosing, not the one chosen for you by others.

Now, here's a word of caution: be prepared for pushback. We all struggle with our desire for control, and one of the main things we love to try to control is other people. But just like we can't control other people, they can't control us.

If we look back at the Issa Rae story through another lens, her father had unset expectations of her. He was vocal in his communication about what he expected from his daughter when it came to her career goals, but his expectations were unrealistic—*and it was his job, not hers, to manage his feelings about his disappointment.*

Yes, I know this runs counter to what we're taught, but as I've said from the beginning, how we've always lived isn't working for us anymore. It's up to us to choose to be responsible for ourselves—for our own goals, for our own happiness—and to respect the people in our lives enough to let them do the same.

When you decide you're no longer going to live according to the goals that others have set for you, they may challenge you, threaten you, or express how deeply disappointed they are in you. But they can't see what you see about the path you're meant to be on. And truth be told, if you haven't had the courage to face your family or friends in this way yet, deep down you are avoiding the conflict that can come with choosing your own path.

Yes, trying to avoid disappointing people you care about is understandable. But if you're struggling with the need to stand up for yourself, you've got to put it to yourself like this: *If I don't do what they expect, I'm going to disappoint them, which I don't want to do. But if I keep working to avoid disappointing them while every day disappointing myself, can I really live like that?* I'd rather have you disappoint others and be true to yourself than disappoint yourself and never live life free.

THERE'S NOTHING MORE DISAPPOINTING THAN A LIFE UNFULFILLED.

Not to mention, it's a fantasy that you can just put someone else and their goals for your life before your own happiness, without any consequences. Eventually, suppressing your true goals is going to make you resentful, or maybe even bring on some of the negative, self-destructive behaviors we've already discussed.

A brief aside for those of you reading this who have realized that you are the one putting fake goals and unrealistic expectations on someone else. You can stop right now. This person whom you care about and have been trying to control might not even realize that you have been putting pressure on them—the pressure to please you and to live up to what you want them to be. It could be a close friend, your child, your significant other, a family member. You know who it is. Let them be free to live. It's okay if they disappoint you. It's their life.

This is also true for employers. Even though you are paying your employees and, of course, have expectations about their performance, you are not their God, and you don't always know what's best for them. Give them the freedom to explore who they are and what they are created to do. And I challenge you to support them every step of the way. If they do things you don't like, pray for them instead of judging them. I urge you: anyone you're guilty of trying to control, let them live free.

LIFE IS TO BE LIVED

A powerful example of someone creating goals that are true for them and no one else is the hip-hop trailblazer and accomplished singer-songwriter Lauryn Hill. She achieved massive success with her breakout group, The Fugees, and especially with her 1998 debut solo album, *The Miseducation of Lauryn Hill*, which has sold more than 19 million copies worldwide. But she hasn't released another studio album for more than two decades.

Lauryn finally acknowledged the impact of the expectations that had hung over her since her early triumph in a personal essay published on Medium in late August 2018. Rather than apologizing for disappointing her fans by choosing a path other than that of reliable pop icon, she expressed a remarkable confidence in her own right to live free of anyone else's expectations about her creativity or productivity. She declared herself free to set her own expectations, decide her own goals, and steer her own direction in life, always and forever: "I reject being pigeonholed or pinned down by someone else's uninformed concept of me. . . . Where I am in one chapter of my life isn't necessarily where I'll be in the next chapter. . . . Life is to be lived, it's not a full-time performance you put on for others."

Truer words have never been spoken. You can't live passively, setting only safe goals and making only those decisions approved by others, just so no one will ever have anything critical to say about you. **Life is to be *lived*.** Your goals should be the sails that power you toward your own next chapter—one that's authentic and meaningful to you and only you.

I bet there's at least one person in your life right now who always seems to veto your inspirations or has a reason why you shouldn't do something. Ask yourself:

- Are my fears about making a big change in my professional life due to negative feedback I have consistently received from a family member or friend?
- What goals do I need to create that will help me to live the life I want?

YOU CONTROL THE NOW BUT NOT ALWAYS THE WHEN

When trying to set real career goals, most of us have a blind spot around the timetables required to meet those goals. In the case of that hypothetical promotion we've talked about, it might not happen for years, even though you pray it will happen tomorrow. As Hofstadter's Law says:

"IT ALWAYS TAKES LONGER THAN YOU EXPECT."

The present is now; the future is when. In order to have the when you desire, you have to maximize the now you control. Even if you are blessed enough to work in the right field and to be gifted at what you do, making it possible to set realistic expectations about your career path, you still don't always control the exact time line for the achievement of those goals. Don't render your otherwise realistic goal unrealistic by putting an improbable timetable on it.

Instead, seek out accurate information about how long it usually takes to accomplish your professional goal, or to at least see a tangible improvement.

A good way to start managing your time line for your goals is to ask yourself:

- What's my biggest professional goal, and when do I expect to achieve it?
- What's one short-term professional goal, and when do I expect to achieve it?
- Is my expectation realistic? What research have I done to determine this?
- Will these goals still be meaningful to me if it takes much longer to accomplish them?

It also bears mentioning that, during unprecedented times like the pandemic of 2020, or whenever there is turmoil, careers and entrepreneurial dreams may be temporarily sidelined. If you've been laid off or had to close your business, please go easy on yourself. Your first priority is stabilizing your emotions as best as you can and processing the pain of the losses you've experienced. After you tend to yourself emotionally, you can then begin to assess what you can do to rebuild your life and career.

When our regular existence is upended, it can be a great opportunity for shifting your focus to smaller, short-term goals you never had time to work on before. Even just dusting off your résumé and giving it a polish can be a productive step in the right direction. The overall rebuild may take years. That's okay. Remember, you don't control when things will be back to how you want them to be, but you do control what you do now, in service of getting there.

THE SECRET TO ACHIEVING YOUR GOALS

Set goals that lift you up by stretching you a little, without discouraging you. Being able to do so is the key to hope, happiness, and peace.

I don't want you to set only safe goals. I want you to set professional goals that energize and excite you. But as we've already established, both unrealistic expectations and fake goals are huge sources of unhappiness, and they could easily be avoided in most cases. So, before you set a professional goal and start to move toward it, identify which of your expectations around this goal are too high, too low, or just right.

I evaluate all of my goals by asking this important question: *Is this goal too high?* By that I mean, no matter how hard I work and how much help I enlist, is what I want impossible? Or even just so unlikely that it's probably not going to happen? If so, I remind myself: *You are just setting yourself up for failure. And you are potentially taking time and energy away from real goals that could actually improve your life if you applied yourself to them instead.*

You need to identify a goal that is within your control, even if it's a stretch. Then ask yourself if there's anyone you need to communicate with about your goal, to better its chances of coming to fruition (just as you do when setting expectations). Then turn your focus from the goal itself to your process. Keep your focus on the process until that goal is met. Usually, your process will need to be tweaked and revamped along the way as you gain new information about what's working, and what's not, in the service of your goal. Over and over, I've used these steps to achieve my goals. The more reality you can bring to your goals, the greater probability there is that you will achieve them. There's nothing pessimistic about this approach; you can still be optimistic and realistic at the same time.

As we've already discussed, the results will be so much better when we're clear on what kinds of choices we're making to achieve any career goal, and why. We all get to decide for ourselves what motivates us and where to put our time, energy, and focus.

BECOME A BETTER BOSS

Workplaces have their own rules, and being aware of them is a major part of functioning successfully in your career. Often you have to set and manage your professional goals in conjunction with your coworkers and bosses, some of whom have similar goals and some of whom have their own agendas. This definitely makes the whole enterprise trickier. But there are many constructive ways in which you can harmonize your goals with those of your coworkers.

Let's say you're in a leadership role. You've earned this position for many good reasons, including greater experience, which has made you more capable of multitasking, hitting deadlines, and handling the pressures of your job.

Maybe there's someone on your team who shows great potential but isn't as developed yet. If you hold them to the exact same standards you have for yourself, they will inevitably make some missteps. They don't have the same skill level or experience you do. You could actually kill this colleague's potential, and maybe even drive them out of their job, by expecting too much and setting goals for them too high, without the proper training or mentorship.

> **THE FASTEST WAY A LEADER CAN DEMORALIZE A TEAM IS TO SET GOALS AT A LEVEL SO HIGH THAT TEAM MEMBERS FEEL LIKE THEY CAN NEVER MEET THEM.**

Now, I'm not saying bosses shouldn't have clear and significant expectations of their employees or teams. (Trust me, I have serious expectations of everyone who works for me.) If bosses had no expectations of their employees, workplaces would soon devolve into chaos and nothing would be accomplished. But those expectations must be set before they can be translated into goals. A good leader establishes ambitious but achievable goals that will stretch their team and help their individual team members to grow, but are not so high that their spirits are crushed. This is something I learned through experience earlier in my career when I undertook the search for the "perfect" assistant.

My odyssey began back in 2003, when I was a studio executive at Sony Pictures Entertainment. I loved the job, but one of my biggest challenges was finding an assistant who could keep up with me (or so I thought). I was going through assistants as often as Michael Jordan changed shoes (every game). The problem, as far as I could see, was that my assistants weren't doing things the way I needed them to be done, I became frustrated, and then I quickly became convinced they were hopeless in the role. Soon, I was interviewing the next candidate. This became an issue: I was one of the youngest executives, with the most potential at the company, but I also had the highest assistant turnover rate, which was unsustainable and made me look bad.

My bosses brought in a professional coach to work with me. After some discussion, we came to an important realization: When I'd entered the entertainment industry as an intern for the company that managed Will Smith, Jada Pinkett Smith, and Jennifer Lopez, I worked for people with very high standards and expectations. For them, it was either sink or swim. There was no learning curve, no weekly check-in, not even any clear instruction of what was expected of me. They didn't care about my feelings. They weren't unkind people. They were just very focused on getting the job done, and they were under a lot of pressure themselves. So I was supposed to figure out what I needed to do and then do it quickly, and perfectly, and to do this again and again and again, with all different types of tasks, in a very fast-paced environment.

Well, because of the type of personality I have, I took on that challenge, and I thrived. I swam and then some. That experience, and the skills I developed, ultimately propelled my success in Hollywood. I had figured out all of that on my own and made it through that testing ground. So my expectation was that anyone working for me *should be able* to figure it out as well, and to decipher what I needed from them, without any special direction from me. I wasn't even as difficult to work for as my former bosses, I thought. So what was the problem?

Using the tools and perspective I have now, I can see that while I had expectations for my assistants, they were unrealistic—they were not set properly. Without ever stopping to analyze the likelihood of a good outcome, or whether I was being fair, I'd based my expectations on the incredibly high standards that I had put on myself and made them the standards my assistants would live or die by. I'd also skipped another important step in setting expectations: I had not communicated them to my assistants. Even if my expectations were probably unattainable for them, I should have given them a better chance of meeting my demands by clearly explaining them. At the time, my coach diagnosed the issue this way: "You can't expect them to do what you did, because everybody is different. So, you can't project your expectations onto them."

As soon as I heard it spoken that simply, I got it. That statement made so much sense to me—I'd created a standard, based on my own experiences, that wasn't actually realistic (or fair). I had to learn to differentiate between my own personal standards, under which I thrive, and those required for my assistants to do a good job. Once I did this, I was able to set my expectations properly.

The first step was to assess what was reasonable to expect of the best possible assistant and to let go of the rest. Next, I had to clearly communicate my expectations to my assistant. With each successive assistant, I've gotten better at articulating my needs, which have become more grounded. Any turnover that has happened more recently has been for reasons other than my previously unset (and unfair) expectations. And when I consider all of my former assistants at Sony and reevaluate their performance through my current, more accurate lens, I can see that several would have actually been great assistants. If I had known how to properly set my expectations at the time, those assistants, and maybe some others as well, could have totally handled the job.

Here's an important distinction that has helped me evolve my leadership skills the clearer I've become on it, and it will help you as well. I still have significant personal and professional expectations—I still want to achieve a lot in my life and impact the world positively, and I still want to do the things I care about well. But those expectations and goals are mine, and they shouldn't become the expectations and goals I put on my staff. They don't have to share my goals and expectations in order to do a good job for me. I've learned that everyone is wired differently. Even though someone's professional drive may not be the same as mine, that doesn't make them a bad person or bad employee.

The key to improving your relationship with your employees is to improve your relationship with yourself and be easier on yourself, carefully set your expectations, and then acknowledge that your expectations are *your* expectations. They should not become the de facto standards for everyone else, not even for those you are paying to work for you.

This was a huge professional and personal breakthrough for me: making a distinction between my own professional expectations and my company expectations. It's easy to mix up the two. What you expect of yourself is not always good to expect of those who work for you. Maybe when you were the same age as your current employees you had the capacity to figure stuff out without somebody walking you through it, like you have to do for them. That's why you have what you have—your capacity is different. You are in that position for a reason. It is unproductive to expect those who work for you to have the same capacity you do. We're all built differently, and that's ultimately what helps a team win.

Can you imagine if, during the Jordan era of the Chicago Bulls, all the players played like Jordan and had the exact same skill set he had? They would have never won a championship, because a team needs different players to play varied roles. And when those differences are appreciated and even celebrated, a team can go to the next level.

Lastly, remember, when you are the boss, communication is always key. Be very clear about your goals and the division of labor. If it is obvious that something is not going to happen as quickly as you'd hoped, don't become so frustrated that you allow your displeasure to disrupt your communication. If a goal needs to be realigned or reassigned, bring your team into the process and you will be more likely to achieve it, no matter what comes your way.

As I've said before and I'll say again, I am very much a work in progress in this area. It's like I'm writing the book I needed to read. As I work on this material and think about these concepts, it helps me to continually release unrealistic professional expectations and set realistic expectations (and goals) in their place. I am forever reminding myself: *The more I can encourage myself to bring an ease to everything I do, and a sense of peace to my life, no matter the outcome, the better able I am to lead others to do the same.* It's not always easy for me, but when I practice this, it actually lets me enjoy work more and get more out of everyone on my team—in contrast to allowing my high ambitions to drag me down, as well as everyone who works with me.

CHAPTER 13 Expectation Examinations

1. What are the top three goals in your life right now? For each goal, ask yourself: Is this goal fake? Realistic? Or unrealistic?

2. Are any of your goals based on external pressure from your family or any other source in your life? Is there a way to reframe the goal so it will be authentic to you, or should it be released?

3. Are your goals realistic? If not, can you tweak them to be more realistic—for example, by extending the time frame in which you expect something to happen?

4. Are there any goals you've been afraid to go for because you doubted you could make them happen? Is there a way you could bring a goal within reach, say, by taking a class?

5. If you are working on a team, what are the collective goals you are pursuing? How could you revamp your teamwork to produce better results?

14

TO SUCCEED YOU MUST EXCEED

You better open your mind. You gotta read between the lines.

—AALIYAH

Much unhappiness has come from things left unsaid.

—LEO TOLSTOY

If you want to succeed in your job, or even to just stay employed, setting your own professional expectations isn't the only thing that matters. As long as you are collecting a check from your boss, what they expect of you is highly important and can't be disregarded, even if you don't like it or feel moved to do something else.

Hear me clearly on this:

UNDERSTANDING, MEETING, AND THEN
EXCEEDING THE EXPECTATIONS OF THE PERSON
YOU WORK FOR ARE THE KEYS FOR ACCELERATION
AND SUCCESS IN YOUR CAREER.

In the previous chapter, I gave you some insights on how to become a better boss. In this chapter, I offer strategies for successfully dealing with your boss, whether or not they're good, and whether or not you like them.

The most challenging part of your job isn't the work itself. It's the many on-the-job expectations that are implied or unspoken. How do you meet or exceed your boss's expectations if they've never been clearly communicated? To succeed you must learn to hear the unspoken.

BECOME ADDICTED TO INFORMATION

You've heard the saying: "What you don't know won't hurt you." When it comes to your career progression, this is one of the most ridiculous, dangerous, and false statements ever.

IGNORANCE IS A PROFESSIONAL LIABILITY.

What your boss knows, but you don't, will hurt you. For example, what they know about the requirements of your job, their mandates related to how you do your job, and even their feelings about you can hurt you if you aren't aware of them. One of the critical questions you need to consistently ask yourself is: *What don't I know?* This could be what you don't know about your job, your performance, or your industry. Any area where you are professionally underinformed or misinformed is a blind spot that, if left unresolved, can derail your entire career.

INFORMATION IS THE ANTIDOTE FOR IGNORANCE.

First things first, you've got to be on the hunt for information. When I was coming up in Hollywood, one of my friends used to call me "nosy" because I was always asking questions. I told her, "I'm not nosy, I'm just addicted to information."

An important first step in accepting greater accountability for your job responsibilities is to make sure you're crystal clear on what they are. As much as you can, find out what's expected of you. Even when it seems like it's obvious, there's always the possibility for misunderstanding and disconnect unless all aspects of your job and its responsibilities are spelled out clearly. How do you gain this information?

If it isn't spelled out for you, don't be afraid to ask questions. Lose your pride right now. I've seen people remain unclear about what's expected of them because they were afraid to ask a question that might make them seem dumb in front of their boss. I'd rather see your boss be frustrated with your question, yet still answer it (giving you the information you need to do your job well), than see you never asking it and being left at a professional disadvantage.

Just think back to when I didn't get promoted after the success of *The Karate Kid*. What if I had a time machine and could go back and properly set my expectations? This time, before we had filmed a single scene, I would have asked my bosses for a meeting, and I would have sat down with them and been very direct. I would have said something like, "I love working for this company and the opportunities it has provided me to learn and grow. I'm eager to move up the ranks, take on even more responsibility and hopefully make an even bigger contribution to the company. Do you think, if *The Karate Kid* is successful and profitable, it's realistic for me to expect I'll get promoted?"

I had already set the expectation that this promotion was a given.

But I hadn't stopped to take that crucial step along the way—to assess if this expectation was realistic. To do so, I needed direct information from my boss. I could have saved myself so much heartache by asking my boss if it was realistic for me to expect a promotion if the movie performed well. But it didn't occur to me to ask for that information at the time. Instead, I made an incorrect assumption. And as a result, I was devastated when I didn't get what I was expecting. Can you see how much easier it would have made my life if I'd simply asked?

Information, excellence, and experience are your greatest professional assets. To become addicted to information, you must seek it out at all costs. The first step is usually to go to your boss directly. If it would be appropriate, make an appointment. Come prepared with questions to gain the information you need. In order to make sure you *really* understand what's expected of you, begin the conversation with a quick summary of what you see as your position's main responsibilities and priorities. Then ask your boss if your assessment is accurate, or if there are other areas where they'd like you to focus instead.

Don't be afraid to ask follow-up questions. Better to make the most of your boss's time so you can leave your meeting with the intel you need to create meaningful improvements. This is also something that could be done during your annual performance review (if your company has them). Be sure to actually listen and take notes. And by the way, these are great tools for any meeting you have on the books—if you come prepared and work on being a good listener, you're likely to make a strong impression.

Another important step is to realize that your boss isn't necessarily the only person of power in your workplace. Be savvy about who's really running the show. You'll do your job better if you're not afraid to ask a more experienced colleague for advice about what's expected of you and to seek their counsel on how to meet these expectations. I made a habit of doing this when I was an executive. I would fre-quently question more experienced colleagues on how to do a better job and to gain information on how to navigate the politics of a given situation. Some of them became mentors on whom I continue to rely to this day, even though we no longer work together. I can't tell you how many times they've helped me through tough decisions or rocky patches in my professional life.

Consider seeking a mentor of your own. I'm often asked how to do so, and I know how frustrating it can be when you haven't been able to find one for yourself. Don't fret, you can attract the right mentor simply through your sheer passion, work ethic, positive attitude, and commitment to your craft. There was no one mentor in my life I sought out. I pursued the career path I was drawn to, with excellence and enthusiasm, and all the mentors I needed were ones I encountered while on that path.

Of course, you can seek out mentorship more directly. Yet the qualities that will inspire someone to mentor you always remain the same. Also, don't limit your search. If a mentor isn't revealed to you at your job, you can also receive virtual mentorship—people you never actually meet but whose work provides you with the guidance you need to inspire and teach you.

In order to better position yourself for greater success, ask yourself:

- What would my boss say are my position's three most important duties? (If you can't answer this question, you're in trouble and need to find out ASAP.)
- In addition to my boss, who else in my workplace can I turn to for help?
- Are there ways in which I could improve my communication style?
- Is there someone within my company or my field who might mentor me?

LEARN YOUR BOSS

Now, I've got some challenging news for you. Even if you have a direct conversation with your superior and it goes well, they probably still have expectations of you that they didn't voice. Why? How? It's not because they are playing mind games. (Well, some bosses do play mind games, but in my experience, most don't.) It's that there are things they expect that they may not even be aware of to communicate to you, or that they have expectations they don't feel they *need* to communicate.

I know this may sound complicated, but stay with me. There are some bosses who are horrible at communication. (Ever worked for one of those? If you're working for someone like this right now, I feel your pain.) If you ask them directly what they expect, they may stumble, or even become flustered; they also just may not be accustomed to fully articulating their expectations. Some bosses may be unwilling to go over every expectation. Truth be told, they may have many of them, but assume that you already know them, so they don't necessarily have to communicate them to you. This is why you must learn your boss. There's a scripture that says, "You must study to show yourself approved."

You notice I didn't say, "Get to know your boss." There's a difference between getting to know your boss and learning your boss. Getting to know them is about becoming more acquainted with them personally. Learning them is about becoming clear on how your boss works and what your boss wants. You may never truly know your boss, but you can definitely learn them.

Dr. Marty Nemko touched on this in an article he wrote for *Psychology Today* titled "10 Things Every Employee Must Do." Many of the items on his to-do list involve communication. And he makes an important distinction: it's not enough to simply communicate—you must do so with finesse. "Manage your boss. Get clear on your boss's priorities and the type of interaction s/he prefers: frequent or infrequent, concise or comprehensive, fact- or feeling-centered, flattering, neutral, or critical. The latter, alas, is rare, even among managers who claim to welcome criticism."

One of the best ways to learn your boss is to observe them. When you spend too much time focused only on what you want to accomplish, you could be missing important information that your boss is communicating. What questions is your boss asking of you or your team? What are your boss's priorities? What does your boss tend to focus on in meetings? If you can't answer these questions, you are lacking vital information. It's being communicated, but you aren't taking it in. This is why I call this skill developing your sixth sense. When your professional sixth sense is heightened because you're taking the time to observe, you can detect the nonverbal expectations of you.

Your boss is always communicating what they want, whether they do it verbally or not. It's up to you to be professionally intuitive, every single day. You have to constantly be observing the dynamics around you and discerning what's really happening in your office and how you can contribute while advancing your own agenda.

Here are some questions to ask yourself:

- What is my boss's disposition and what kind of interactions (meetings, phone calls, emails) do they respond to best?
- What's important to my boss (for example, punctuality, creativity, aggressiveness, process)?
- Do I have any allies within my company who could help me hone my perspective?

THINK OUTSIDE OF YOUR PERSPECTIVE

The real challenge related to developing these types of skills is getting out of our own way. We are so accustomed to seeing things from our own perspective that it is often difficult to put ourselves in other people's shoes. Again, this is not just true of professional relationships. As we'll delve into in the next section, so much tension arises in romantic and family relationships because too often we project our own perspective or desires onto the other person. Learning to achieve greater perspective is always valuable.

Being able to see through someone else's eyes has many benefits beyond just wowing your boss and having a more nuanced approach to problem-solving. It can actually help you achieve goals that were otherwise out of your reach. In a lesson on how perspective can shape our lives in powerful ways, Ryan Holiday draws on a pretty remarkable story from early in George Clooney's career in his book *The Obstacle Is the Way*. Even though George is a huge international star now, when he first tried to break into Hollywood he endured constant rejection. He was fixated on being liked and chosen by producers and casting directors, and when they didn't choose him, he got angry and blamed them for not recognizing his talent.

Then George had the awareness to realize that it wasn't them—it was him. In order to become the actor he believed he already was, he would need to completely flip his perspective. He realized that, when he walked into an audition, solely focused on landing the part, he wasn't seeing the other point of view—how stressful the auditioning process was for these producers and casting agents. They absolutely had to find the perfect person for each role, and they never knew if that perfect person was right around the corner or not.

George began to see auditions as an opportunity to solve this problem for them, not just by being a good actor but also by having an inherent understanding of what the part required and how to deliver it for them—solving all of their problems at once. This new perspective created a new confidence in him—a confidence that projected the message: *They will like me, but I'll be fine if they don't.* As soon as he made this shift, he began landing parts left and right. As Ryan points out, "The difference between the right and the wrong perspective is everything. . . . Where the head goes, the body follows. Perception precedes action. Right action follows the right perspective."

You already know how crucial a healthy, correct perspective is for being successful in life. And of course, the same holds true for your professional life. If you can infer the problems being experienced by your boss and solve them before even being asked to, you are positioning yourself for massive success.

Not only will you deliver results, but you'll also give your boss the feeling of having their needs attended to, which I think is a central desire that we all have, and that too often goes unmet. The best part is that, unlike that promotion that's out of your control, self-mastery and interpersonal finesse are definitely within the realm of what you can control and improve at over time.

COMMUNICATE, COMMUNICATE, AND COMMUNICATE SOME MORE

As you see, communication is a running theme in this book. It's never a one-off, especially at work, where responsibilities and deadlines are constantly arising and shifting. It might be uncomfortable to acknowledge to your boss that you're not going to be able to meet a particular expectation—but do it anyway. It will be so much better to talk about it and see what can be done. Also, by asking for more time, or for a temporary respite from other duties in order to focus all of your attention on this more pressing deadline, or for help from your boss in prioritizing your tasks, you will not only accomplish all of the tasks but gain valuable intel about what's more important—fulfilling this specific responsibility or keeping your overall workload afloat.

As I've already mentioned, I've had challenges with some of my employees in the past. My lightbulb moment came when I realized that I *still* hadn't set my expectations; even though I'd recalibrated them to be realistic, I hadn't communicated them clearly. One day I had an epiphany: *I'm expecting people to understand what I want, but I'm not communicating it effectively to them, and so they're unable to deliver. I can't just assume people will automatically infer the right way to do something if I haven't clearly told them.*

Now I take more time to communicate from the outset of any project. And my employees have a contribution to make too. When something doesn't meet my expectations, we discuss what happened, and I encourage them to explain their perspective. Plus, everyone is given the chance to push back if something doesn't work for them, or to renegotiate if they're not going to be able to accomplish something. We don't always agree on everything, and I'm still the boss, but it's a more collaborative—and ultimately more sustainable—approach.

I've seen that, over time, people who work around me do start to pick up a sense of what I'm expecting from them. But it wouldn't be efficient, or fair, to have that be their sole way of learning their duties. And so I never assume they know my expectations anymore. (Or when I do, I try to catch myself as quickly as possible.) I think that's one of the biggest mistakes we can make: assuming that our perspective is shared by everyone, especially if we're in a leadership role.

If I'm not getting what I want, I know that I have to adjust my process. I start by seeking out places where I can do a better job of communicating. Then I try to complete the extra step of making sure that my communication has been understood. And then, once all of this is clear *and agreed upon by both sides,* I can hold people accountable if they don't meet those properly set expectations. Then and only then will there be consequences. This process might require an uncomfortable conversation, but in the long run it's better for everyone. Maybe I have to diagnose the problem and seek ways to rectify it with the employee. Then, if the issues persist with that individual, maybe it's a sign that there's an incorrect fit and it's time for them to move on.

Whatever the outcome may be, this is a much more productive process than assuming and becoming frustrated. At least in this scenario, there is the chance for improvement and growth—on all sides.

My professional coach, Coach Mo, also helps me in how I communicate, with my employees or with other business associates. Again, there have been so many situations in my professional life when I was sure I was saying something loud and clear, but in actuality my message was muddled, vague, or contradictory. I have put real effort into improving in this area, and Mo has been invaluable in mirroring back to me what she hears me *actually* saying and in helping me think about how my message might be received. Of course, a huge foundational stepping-stone has been all of the work I've done to clarify my expectations and decide whether or not they are realistic so I can focus on communicating those that are realistic to those around me.

There are certain positive qualities I particularly admire, such as hard work, initiative, and follow-through. Everyone values different things, but the people who do well with me have at least some of these qualities and lead with them. In return for the respect and passion they bring to their relationship with me, and the work we do together, I always think about what I can do to help and benefit them by giving them the opportunity to do the things they love to do and helping them to learn, explore, and expand their career.

DON'T JUST MEET EXPECTATIONS, EXCEED THEM

IF YOU ARE TRYING TO GET PROMOTED, YOU CANNOT SIMPLY MEET THE EXPECTATIONS OF YOUR BOSS. YOU MUST EXCEED THEM.

Repeat after me:

TO SUCCEED I MUST EXCEED!

After you have identified what your boss's expectations are, then it's up to you to go above and beyond them. This is a vital lesson that rarely gets spoken about, so I'm helping you decode the real keys to career advancement right now.

Meeting expectations is the standard; that's equivalent to the status quo. Achieving that standard is fine and all, but it's very rare for the status quo to advance your career. Simply doing the minimum required by your job will earn you the paycheck, but exceeding expectations can earn you the corner office.

When you commit to going above and beyond the call of duty, you position yourself for unprecedented success. How? Very few people strive to excel. Most people do the job they're asked to do, and that's it. When you commit to becoming an expectation-exceeder, you put yourself in rare air, and you will be noticed. Whether it comes at your current job or in a new job you gain, success will be yours. Those seeds of excellence will grow, I guarantee it, leading you to the career and life of your wildest dreams. So set your sights above what's required of you each and every day, and you'll live professionally freer than ever before.

CHAPTER 14 **Expectation Examinations**

1. Is there an important conversation you need to have about what you can honestly expect from a situation and what is expected of you—whether it's with your boss or someone on your team at work?

    i. Why have you been avoiding this talk? Are you pretty sure you're not going to receive the answer you want? Even so, remember that it's better to gain information—accurate information—from your boss or colleagues than to live in uncertainty.

    ii. To prepare for this conversation, practice writing down the questions you need to ask the other person, to clarify the present reality and future possibility of that relationship.

2. What is your biggest current source of interpersonal stress at work right now? It could be with your boss, with a colleague, or with anyone close to you on the job. Be really honest with yourself: Are your unrealistic expectations about this person at the root of your frustration? What would be a more realistic expectation of this person's behavior or attitude?

3. Who is one person in your professional life—maybe your boss, your new sales prospect, or your most important client—whose perspective you would benefit from understanding better? What are you able to learn when you put yourself in their shoes?

4. Can you be happy at your current job, or do you need to set yourself free for something new?

15

FEEL YOUR FEELINGS

Your profession is not what brings home your weekly paycheck, your profession is what you're put here on earth to do, with such passion and such intensity that it becomes spiritual in calling.

—Vincent van Gogh

I've gone seventy-nine hours without sleep, creating. When that flow is going, it's almost like a high. You don't want it to stop. You don't want to go to sleep for fear of missing something.

—Dr. Dre

It's all about perspective. As he describes it in his book *Old School Love: And Why It Works,* Joseph "Rev Run" Simmons hit rock bottom at a moment when it would have seemed to most people like his life couldn't have gotten any better. He was in Los Angeles to headline the Forum with Run DMC at the height of their fame. He was feeling pretty high on himself (and literally high) after he checked into the presidential suite at the best hotel (with a brand-new Rolls-Royce parked outside), lit up a joint, and filled the huge jacuzzi tub.

He managed to convince room service to deliver him a gigantic breakfast at lunchtime by dropping his name. He gorged himself, in the tub, while waiting for a *Rolling Stone* reporter to interview him for a cover story. When he opened his door to the three men standing there—the reporter, his weed dealer, and his Rolls-Royce driver—instead of feeling pride and satisfaction, he broke down: "I had this realization: I don't just have things—things have me. . . . All the trappings that came from this talent that God had given me, all the stuff, didn't make me happy, didn't bring me joy, did not fill me up."

In that instant, he had an awakening and realized that his idea of success was totally wrong and empty. What he really needed, to feed his joy, was to have God in his life. Soon after, he became ordained as a minister. And while he didn't stop rapping or retire his mantle as a beloved entertainment figure, he massively shifted his idea of a good and abundant life.

Later in the book, written with his wife, Justine, he sums up the gift of purpose and joy that came with his perspective shift and the profound changes it led him to make, always with his spirit guiding him: "When you're not doing something with the expectation that it should be handed to you, or it should be given to you because of who you are, the entire world opens up to you. It happens because of the love you pour into what you're doing."

Yes, those who are lucky enough to gain such wisdom know it to be true: with fewer expectations, there's so much more room for love, among all the other real riches that pour in. And when you really listen to yourself and what your spirit is calling you to do, you can gain access to a life of true purpose that will make even fame and riches pale by comparison.

To unlock your own feeling of greater purpose, ask yourself:

- If I'm totally honest with myself, what is my heart really calling me to do?
- If money were no object, how would I spend my days?
- Am I living by definitions of success or accomplishment that feel empty? What would be more meaningful for me as a symbol of a life well lived?

HEAR WHAT YOUR SPIRIT IS SAYING

Reverend Run was fortunate. His epiphany was coupled with a plan—to prioritize God and make decisions about his life and career by listening to his spirit. But what if you feel like you haven't received such a clear message? What if you tried to answer the questions above and you're not sure of the answers? How do you learn to listen to what's going on inside of you, so you can find what *you're* called to do in this life?

FIRST OF ALL, SLOW DOWN. YOU'VE GOT TO STOP RUNNING.

You may have been running your whole life, running from what you feel, because you don't know what to do with it, or you're afraid you've gone astray but you don't know where or how. Well, you now have the tools to set your expectations for yourself, and by doing so, to set yourself free. From this moment forward, you're going to start doing everything a little bit differently. Start right away, when you wake up in the morning. Instead of rushing into your day, literally stop, before you do anything else, and ask yourself:

HOW DO I FEEL?

And then, as you go through your day, especially your workday, keep asking yourself:

HOW DO I FEEL?

Do you feel motivated to make progress, even on days that are challenging or involve some tasks that aren't necessarily your favorite? Or do you spend most of your day wishing that you were doing anything other than what you're supposed to be doing?

LISTEN, AND THEN FOLLOW
WHAT YOU'RE HEARING.

As with everything else, you can get better at tuning in to your heart with practice. Dr. Diana Raab, in her *Psychology Today* article "Being in Touch with Our Emotions," suggests some helpful ways to access and connect with your feelings: "Sit in a quiet place and focus on your abdominal area. Center yourself. Place your right hand on your abdomen, and repeat three times, 'Please reveal my true emotions.' Listen for the answers that come to you and write them down. Repeat this exercise as often as needed."

Don't be afraid to face whatever feelings come up for you. If being at your job doesn't feel right, don't suppress that feeling, acknowledge it. Don't be afraid to admit that maybe you've gone the wrong direction in your career, and in your life. It's okay. You can still change your course and chart a new future for yourself that will be of your choosing.

The only way this moment could be a negative is if you never acknowledge what you're really feeling about where you are right now. The only real potential failure could be reaching the end of your life and realizing that you never really lived your life, *and you could have.* Can you accept that as your future fate? I'll answer for you: No, of course not! You deserve and can have so much more than that. The choice is yours.

Ask yourself:

- What am I hearing inside of myself that I'm not listening to?
- What changes do I know I've got to make that I haven't made yet?
- What am I afraid will happen if I admit I'm unhappy and choose a new job or life?

Before we go any further, I want to stop and acknowledge the lasting impact of the Covid-19 pandemic of 2020. It was a disastrous, heartbreaking moment for so many careers and businesses all over the world, with tens of millions of people losing their jobs. Maybe it forced you to make a career change or look for a new job. Or maybe you managed to stay employed through the pandemic but something else unexpected occurred, and now you're unemployed. Let's be honest, when the unexpected happens, it can be hard to remain hopeful.

If your professional landscape has suddenly become uncertain, I understand that you may have difficulty connecting to the inherent hopefulness in many of the questions I am posing. That's okay. You must take a moment to acknowledge how you feel. Grieve your losses. Address your anxiety. Cry your tears.

Now, here's how you regain hope. Mory Fontanez, a renowned transformation coach, offered this advice, which I love, in Heather Taylor's *Business Insider* article "7 Reasons That It's Time to Change Jobs During the Coronavirus Pandemic," which was published at the height of the pandemic: "Crisis is an opportunity. It asks us to pause and look deeply and honestly at all the things we have been doing day in and day out without really thinking about whether those things fulfilled us, played on our strengths, or aligned with our own purpose."

Maybe you didn't pray for this wake-up call, but maybe it could turn out to be a blessing in unexpected ways. If you find yourself looking for a job, ask yourself if you really want to stay in the same field. Maybe it's time to seek a position that would be more in line with what you've always really dreamed of doing. If your world has changed drastically, can you see a new opportunity you could pursue that maybe never occurred to you before?

By asking yourself all of these questions, you can flip a negative into a positive and regain hope—not to mention your career path. Whatever you decide, don't hold yourself to the status quo. At a moment when it can be difficult to even define what's realistic, setting your expectations will require flexibility and self-compassion.

COUNT THE COST

Once again, I'm not asking you to do anything that I haven't done first myself. In fact, I've had several moments when my life was transformed completely by what I found when I looked deep inside myself—at my real self, at my real path. In my case, these conversations happen with God, and He helps me dig down and find the answers for myself.

The first time this happened to me, as I told the story in my first book, *Produced by Faith*, it was early 2002 and I was working at Overbrook Entertainment, the production company started by Will Smith and his manager James Lassiter. I had worked my way up from an intern position in 1996 to James Lassiter's second assistant in 2000. But after two years in this position, I hit a wall. Hard. I knew my next step was to become a junior executive in film development, but at that time there was no movement at all toward that goal at Overbrook. I forced myself to be honest with myself—in the same ways I'm encouraging you to be honest with yourself—and faced the truth: the career advancement I was hoping for was never going to happen at this company.

How do you know if it's time to move on from a job? For me, the epiphany was swift and clear, but that's not always the case. One of the best methods for making this determination is to do a cost-benefit analysis, which the investment news website TheStreet defines as "a strategy used by businesses and individuals to weigh the potential outcome of an action in order to make a decision." You evaluate whether the cost of being at your current job is greater than the benefit you're receiving from it. If it is, then it's time to go. If it is not, then stay put.

To be sure I was clear on my current situation, I did a cost-benefit analysis of my experience as an assistant. I found that the cost definitely outweighed the benefit. I wasn't growing, I felt like I didn't matter, and it had gotten to the point where it became difficult for me to go into the office. I knew it was time to go, but I was afraid to quit my job. So finally, in desperation, I had it out with God in a stall of the men's room at Overbrook. I was telling Him that I needed Him to move on my job *that day*. I couldn't take it anymore.

Well, that very day, James pulled me aside and told me that while he and Will liked me and knew that I was going to have a great career, the company was changing, and they knew I'd hit a wall. So they were going to help me find a job elsewhere. *Wow.* God really was listening. *But*—this meant I also had to find a new job. During this period of several months, I looked everywhere I possibly could, submitted résumé after résumé, and completed interview after interview, but no job came.

I was at my wits' end, and that's when I heard a message from

Bishop T. D. Jakes that changed my career. He preached a sermon about stepping out on faith. So, with no safety net in place, I officially quit my job and gave my two weeks' notice at Overbrook. People thought I was crazy, but I knew I had to move in faith. It was only then that the next career door opened for me. On my first day of unemployment, I was offered a job at a major production company, in the very role I had been seeking all along—a junior executive in film development.

Yes, it was great that I was offered the position I had been striving for, but even more crucial was the fact that I'd found a new job where the benefit far outweighed the cost. I knew this because of the cost-benefit analysis I had performed during my dark night of the soul. This was priceless information that I would never lose sight of again.

I'd argue that as long as you are growing and learning at work, even if it's not your dream job or where you know you're meant to end up, the benefits are still outweighing the costs. You should keep this position. On the other hand, when you reach the point where you know that every day you stay is a day that is hurting your progress, then the cost outweighs the benefits. And you are paying this cost with your time, growth, money, peace, energy, and motivation. That's when it's time to move on.

So ask yourself:

- What are the benefits of my current job versus the costs?
- Is there an obvious point in the future (at the end of a project, for example) when it's clear the costs will start to outweigh the benefits? Can I plan to leave then?
- If the costs already outweigh the benefits, can I commit to a six-month plan to leave?

The second time I had an aha moment about where I was meant to be in life versus where I currently was, I was on the set of the *Karate*

Kid remake. I know I've already talked about this film as an important transition point in my life. But now I'll tell the deeper story—about what happened inside of me, and the series of revelations that led me to where I am today.

It all started with God speaking to me while I was watching the Smith family play around on set. I had this epiphany: *This is not my movie. I am working on it, but it is someone else's creation. What am I going to create? What is inside of me?*

It's really tempting to become so invested in and involved with something that you do it at the expense of what's really going on inside yourself. At that moment, I realized that this was not my movie. I was only servicing this movie. My cost-benefit analysis had shown me that I was still benefiting a great deal from being of service to that film, and from my job, but God had inspired me to ask deeper questions of myself: *Who are you? What's in you? If you are so focused on this movie and not on yourself, you're going to miss what's really going on in you, and what I'm trying to do through you.* After asking these questions, I clearly came to understand that my days as an executive were numbered.

It actually took five years, from that epiphany to when I finally gave my notice to my boss at Sony Pictures Entertainment. During that time, I committed myself to learning as much as I could. I used my job as an opportunity to incubate my dream of starting my own production company. I sought out even more knowledge about how to make all types of movies.

I also put my other talents and passions to use. I wrote my first book. I built up my speaking profile. I began to do television appearances. Meagan and I started dating, and ultimately we got married. My life started growing in amazing ways. But I never stopped listening to that voice inside of myself. I never stopped looking for my opportunity to take my leap of faith and go out on my own.

That moment came in 2014, when I was a producer on a film called

Heaven Is for Real. The movie came out, made $30 million in its first five days, and eventually made more than $100 million worldwide. At that point, I finally knew I had done all I could do at Sony, and I felt released to start my own company. I had built up all of these other areas of my life that I would need to draw on for what came next. I was ready.

After the success of the movie, I set up a meeting with Amy Pascal, the chairman of Sony Pictures at the time. We had a fantastic conversation. She was beyond pleased with the performance of the film. I knew this was the time to take my shot, so right in the middle of our conversation I said, "It's time for me to leave. It's always been my dream to run my own company. It's time for me to start my own production company, and I want you to fund it. I want you to give me a production deal."

After a moment of thinking about it, she said yes. And that was the start of Franklin Entertainment.

Yep, you heard me right—it took *five years* between my epiphany about needing to strike out on my own and the time when I was actually ready to take the leap. So I'm not in any way telling you to quit your job tomorrow. What I'm suggesting is that, today, you start the process of believing in yourself and your future. Look for all the benefits in your cost-benefit analysis of your current job and do everything you can to better position yourself.

Instead of showing up every day with your focus on how much you hate your job and how it's only good for paying your bills, shift your perspective. This will immediately transform your dead-end job into the springboard for what you're meant to be doing. If there are any skills you know you'll need in the next chapter of your life that you could learn at your current job, commit yourself to gaining that knowledge while you're there. If there's nothing more for you to learn there, take comfort in the fact that you have a steady paycheck. Build a nest egg. Use that money to finance the research and development phase of your next big move, whether it's buying books, taking classes, or actually launching a side hustle that will become your main undertaking. Do this just one step at a time, slowly if you need to, and you will literally set yourself free, even if your day-to-day life still looks exactly the same from the outside.

UNLOCK YOUR POTENTIAL

Even after you've become clear on your true purpose and the goals that will lead you there, reprogramming yourself and recalibrating your dreams is not an overnight pursuit. Rather, it's a daily practice. The trick is to lean into the power you can amass from taking that crucial first step—looking inside, trusting your instincts—and then building from there.

Make it a habit to listen to yourself with greater self-confidence and trust than ever before. A powerful exercise to help you strengthen this muscle is found in the classic, bestselling self-help book *What to Say When You Talk to Yourself* by Dr. Shad Helmstetter, which is in its forty-fifth printing after more than thirty years of publication in more than seventy countries. The foundational method of Dr. Helmstetter's approach can produce a profound inner shift: "If you had just the right kind of successful new mental programs, would you be doing the same thing for a living that you are doing now? . . . And, with different preparation or conditioning, what could your future hold? Would it be the same as your future holds for you today, or would it be better?"

We can always reprogram ourselves, just as we did with our internal software in chapter 2. Here are some questions that can help you discern what your best next move will be. Ask yourself:

- What are my natural gifts?
- What can I do well with minimal effort?

- If I forget the practical path that I felt obligated to take, what are my true passions?
- What have I always been curious about?

Obviously, some of these questions will resonate more for you than others. But I'd also challenge you to not just go with the easy answers. Take the time to dig deeper and find out what's really inside of you. The breakthroughs you experience from stretching yourself in this way may provide new and surprising insights. Whatever answer you land on as your true path, commit to making at least one proactive change in that direction. Purpose is like anything else in life: it is built slowly, one positive decision or set expectation at a time.

WHEN IT'S OKAY TO QUIT

Yes, be strategic about taking the next step in your life. But eventually, as happened in my own journey on several different occasions, the time comes when you must simply go for it. I know in our culture there's a stigma around quitting, and I definitely don't support giving up on something simply because it's hard. But if you're too proud, stubborn, or embarrassed to admit you're on the wrong path (especially the wrong career path), that's just another way of living a life that's not really of your choosing. That's a whole lot worse than quitting something you know isn't working for you, especially once you've homed in on what would work better.

> **DON'T EVER QUIT ANYTHING IN A**
> **MOMENT OF ANGER OR FRUSTRATION.**

In my experience, whenever you make decisions out of anger or frustration, you are rashly making the wrong choice. Even if you are

frustrated with your job or angry with your boss on a daily basis, resist the temptation to be reactionary. This is especially true during
moments of economic instability. If you have to stay in a position that
you're not very happy with, and you hate the workplace culture and
are itching to do something else, go easy on yourself. Try to do everything in your power to make the best of your current situation. And
look for any advantages you can find.

This is the time to strategize—to put a game plan in place that
will allow you to move on when you feel it's finally time. Even if you
aren't in a position to quit anytime soon, just the awareness that you
need to do so can motivate you to create your escape hatch (by fresh-
ening up your résumé, inquiring about new job opportunities, making plans to go back to school, and so on). Maybe you give yourself
a year, or six months, and during that time you move forward with
an orderly plan for what comes next. From then on, anytime you are
angry at work, turn your attention to your strategy for leaving and for
getting ahead in your life. And eventually, when everything is lined
up just right—or, as happened for me, when nothing is in place yet
but your spirit speaks, giving you the sign—you will be quite clear
that it's time to go.

When approached with this kind of forethought and self-
control, quitting allows you to release what isn't right while simul-
taneously opening up space to receive into your life what is right.
It can actually be a positive strategic move that makes you even
more likely to succeed, because you had to clear a hurdle to reach
the next chapter of your life. Helen Roe, a business growth strat-
egist and success coach, talks about the benefits of quitting in her
piece "7 Reasons Why Quitting Is Sometimes Your Best Move."
As she points out, "You know when it's time to consider quitting,
when things no longer feel right. . . . It's not about effort. It's about
awareness. . . . There are times when quitting is sometimes your
best move."

DOING THE RIGHT THING ISN'T
ALWAYS THE SAFE THING.

Our feelings are our spiritual and emotional thermometer. As we've discussed, being in touch with how we feel is critical for assessing how we're really doing. Often, we feel uncertain about how to fix the situation, and so we drown out our negative feelings about our career direction. Trust me, I've been there, as you've just read. Both times, however, before I got to the point of quitting, I had to find the courage to really face what I was feeling and to no longer run from it. Being clear on what you feel, where you are, and why it's not working for you will lead you to the place that ultimately will.

CHAPTER 15 Expectation Examinations

1. Can you find greater purpose at your current job, or do you need to move on?

2. Is there another area of the company you work for that aligns better with your passions?

3. Can you make a commitment to yourself that you will find a new, better job or position within a year?

4. Is there a side hustle you could start that would give you an influx of money and joy?

5. What three steps can you put into place today to start moving toward a deeper purpose?

6. Can you free yourself of beliefs and goals that aren't yours, or that no longer serve you, in order to make healthier choices and become your best, truest self?

EPILOGUE

Expectations!

Once you do the work of setting your expectations properly, you set the stage for the life you always believed you could have.

The shift is really that profound. And that's why this lesson about setting expectations can start a cultural revolution. I've already taught this message in front of thousands, and it receives a response like no other message I've ever taught. Why? Because no matter who we are, or where we are, expectations affect us all. Whether young or old, male or female, single or married, we all have struggled with managing our expectations. It's universal. And this is why I believe this message has struck a powerful chord, and why it will continue to do so.

In fact, after I preached on expectations for the first time at my family's church, Wings of Love in Oakland, it established a new code word that has helped us set our expectations as a family. I was raised by my mother, my grandmother, and my grandmother's seven sisters. I had a front-row seat for watching how my grandmother and great-aunts would all coerce one another to do things they didn't really want to do. Whatever one of the sisters asked, the recipient of that request was expected to do it. This led to some significant resentments and tension in our family. The idea of "family first" had made them feel obligated to do things even if it wasn't in their heart to do them.

However, after hearing my sermon, it's like something broke free in my family. Once they got the revelation about setting expectations, anytime someone in the family would ask someone else to do something they didn't want to do, they would put a finger in the air and blurt out:

"EXPECTATIONS!"

Instantly, both people got it. Usually, they laughed. What they were communicating was, *Wait a minute, don't put your expectation on me.* No one got bent out of shape or had their feelings hurt. It actually helped them talk through the request and what could be expected and what couldn't. It may seem trivial, but this practice helped to change (and improve) communication in our family forever.

You know how it is with families: it can be extremely challenging to speak up when someone you love wants you to do something you may not want to do. So now, having a method to sort through all of this, without ruffling any feathers, was truly transformational.

Setting expectations doesn't always have to be a big production, centered on a heavy conversation. It can become an automatic response, just like when you used to automatically say yes to whatever was asked of you, without weighing its potential cost.

Usually, with members of my family, a bit more will be said on the matter, along the lines of: "Don't have that expectation. I can't meet it." Or if it's a more serious request, the conversation will probably be a little more nuanced, like, "Hold on, I'm not sure if you can expect that from me. Let's talk this through."

There are a million ways to have this conversation, and every family and relationship has its own unique communication style. But now you have a universal tool for saying a qualified no, whether you're responding to a family member, your spouse or significant other, a friend or neighbor, or whoever. Instead of ever again feeling obligated or pressured to do something you really don't feel called to do, and then resenting this person for "making" you do it, use your new code word: *Expectations!*

ACCOMPLISH MORE

Remember how unset expectations can lead you to create fake goals, which can cause you to waste time and energy going in the wrong direction? Setting expectations is the exact antidote for that.

SET EXPECTATIONS HAVE ANOTHER BENEFIT:
YOU ACCOMPLISH MORE.

How? When your expectations are set and firmly based in reality, you can actually be more productive. Why? You're not living or thinking unrealistically anymore, or delaying what you're supposed to do today, because you're too focused on what you hope will happen tomorrow. You're no longer waiting around, expecting somebody else to do something for you. You are clear on the fact that this is your life, and you're taking control.

Also, you're not losing any time or energy to the negative emotions you might have had before, when you were frustrated or angry, expecting someone else to do something that they were never going to do, since you had never communicated your expectation or they had never agreed to it. Instead, you can now hold others accountable. You can actually put processes into place to move you from where you are to where you want to be, individually and collectively. Inevitably, this clarity of focus and purpose will give you more energy for your goals and help you achieve more, because you are no longer wasting precious energy the way you did when your expectations were running wild.

When you set expectations, you have a chance to be more efficient, to really focus your days, to really utilize your personal power. Everything about the process of setting your expectations can help you free up your energy and hone your ability to be more productive.

GO WITH THE FLOW

IF YOU DON'T BEND, YOU'LL BREAK. IN LIFE YOU MUST BE FLEXIBLE.

In the face of new information, you must be comfortable revamping your expectations if they're going to remain set. For example, during the pandemic, like most of us, I worked remotely, and so did all of my employees. Without having everyone together in the office, I had to acknowledge that it was suddenly a little bit harder to accomplish things. I couldn't expect everything to be completed in the time frame I had originally envisioned. I had to set new expectations that would be realistic, given this new world in which we were all living.

Also, nearly all film and TV productions were temporarily shut down. I had to change my expectations there as well, acknowledging that what I had expected in terms of what movies would be made, and when, was no longer realistic.

The principle here is that, even after you've set your expectations, you shouldn't worship them to the point where you become inflexible. If you're not flexible, you're going to break, personally, spiritually, and possibly even professionally. When you receive new information, don't be afraid to adjust what you're expecting and to set new expectations. That doesn't mean you have to give up your goals. But you might have to shift your expectation for how long it's going to take to meet those goals, and then you might have to adjust your expectations yet again.

It's a fluid process. And flexibility is a work in progress for most of us, since we all have that tendency to want to control everything. We have to devote ourselves to perpetually assessing, revising, and resetting.

To revisit the broken bone analogy, the doctor may set your broken leg and put it in a cast. But then they look at the X-ray and realize it needs to be reset, or it won't heal properly. So they go in, break your leg again, and reset it, to make it grow stronger. The break may hurt in the moment, but it will ultimately help your leg heal properly.

Try not to see this as a bad thing, because it never fails: the moment you set your expectations, your life and God start sending you messages that will shift your path and sometimes force you to reset.

It's like the dream I had to become a producer. I didn't know exactly how that was going to happen. I set my intention—I set my expectation. And as information came in, I adjusted what I was expecting at any given moment. But I still kept the real goal of ultimately becoming a Hollywood producer, and I eventually did it. I had to be flexible on the how and the when.

EXPECT THE UNEXPECTED

You can set your expectations properly and think you've gotten your life all lined up exactly where you want it to be—or at least headed in the right direction, with a good process in place for moving it forward. But life doesn't come with any guarantees that you still won't have moments of frustration or anger. No matter how realistic your expectations are, and how clearly you have communicated them, you will still face setbacks. You will still need to develop, cultivate, and maintain a certain amount of personal resilience in the face of the surprises that life has in store for you, some of them quite unpleasant.

For most of us, 2020 is a perfect example of this phenomenon. When everyone was making their New Year's resolutions back in January, trying to kick off their year in the most positive way possible, we had no idea that we would be on the verge of experiencing one of the biggest challenges in history: Covid-19.

EXPECT THE ROAD OF LIFE TO HAVE UNEXPECTED TURNS.

Things are going to happen to you in life that you can't plan for. And being prepared for that can make you less fearful and more hopeful.

Early in the pandemic, I was asked to do some life coaching sessions with two NBA teams, the Boston Celtics and the Minnesota Timberwolves. I'm a huge basketball fan, so this was an exciting opportunity for me, to work with organizations I greatly admire. But on a more personal level, getting a chance to help these gifted athletes gain some perspective off the court and weather a very difficult time was even more rewarding.

When I led our Zoom sessions together, these players had not played for several months. What they were telling me was that they were feeling lost. They didn't know what to do if they weren't practicing or playing a game. They didn't know who they were if they weren't wearing their jersey, holding down their position on the court, being cheered on by their fans. They were having trouble coping with the unexpected.

I told them: "Basketball may be what you do, but basketball is not who you are. There's more in you than just who you are on the basketball court. The person you are when you're off the court is even more important than the person you are on the court."

Understanding who we are can be our anchor, helping us weather whatever storms life may bring. Too often, we mistake our identity for what we do. As a result, unexpected occurrences in life have a tendency to shake our identity to the core. When we go through tough times, we have to remember that we are who we are, not what we do.

I've found that this understanding helps us endure the unexpected by reassuring us of what we can expect. I want to remind you that you've been through tough times before, and you'll survive tough times again. But even when you do expect the unexpected, you may be wondering how you navigate those surprises, whatever they are, so that they don't completely devastate you.

First, repeat this scripture, Psalm 118:17, aloud, as many times as you need to: "I will not die but live, and will proclaim what the Lord has done." This is a positive affirmation that declares your intent to make it through whatever comes your way, and it's a powerful reminder that you aren't alone; God is walking beside you, every step of the way, every day. So stop speaking doom over your life by focusing only on the potential negatives. This is an affirmation that will help you, no matter what happens. Repeat after me: "I will not die but live!"

Second, think of the caterpillar and the cocoon. Once the caterpillar goes into the cocoon, it's in a tight, dark, and extremely lonely place. However, I want to remind you that, even in these difficult circumstances, the caterpillar is transforming. Going through this challenging process is essential for the caterpillar to reach its full potential. When the time is right, that caterpillar will emerge, transformed as a butterfly. Just like the caterpillar in the cocoon, every challenge you face is a new opportunity for your own radical and positive personal transformation.

LEARN TO EMBRACE UNEXPECTED MOMENTS.

When I look back over my life and consider the periods when I've been the most fulfilled, I know it's because I leaned into the surprises that were thrown my way. I also tried to be honest with myself about what was going on, how I felt about it, and how I might modify my expectations to deal with it.

Which brings up another important point: personal development, especially during trials in your life, will benefit you in all areas of your life. Read books. Seek mentors. Perfect your practice, whatever it may be. Work on becoming a better you. It's the only thing you truly control, especially during times of uncertainty.

UNEXPECTED EVENTS CAN REVEAL UNEXPECTED GIFTS

If you find yourself facing a sudden challenge that is testing your resilience, no matter how severe it may be, stay strong.

DON'T PLAY THE VICTIM. PLAY THE VICTOR.

YOU ARE NOT THE VILLAIN OF YOUR STORY.
YOU ARE THE HERO.

Even when the unexpected happens, that does not mean you lose the power of choice. We all can decide how we react, and how we live, even when we're facing down tragic events. And if this moment in your life is challenging, there is still a benefit to be found.

EVERYTHING THAT HAPPENS *TO* US
IS REALLY HAPPENING *FOR* US.

Even in the most difficult situation, ask yourself: *Where is the gift?* Because if you look for it, in my experience, you will always find it. I know it can be tough in the moment.

I was nine when my father died, and the blow was devastating. It sure didn't feel like a gift. Even now, more than thirty years later, it's still difficult. But there was undoubtedly a gift in that loss, one that literally changed the course of my life forever. It gave me the passion for inspiration, and it's this conviction that has fueled my purpose in life.

In the immediate wake of my father's passing, when I was in deep grief, the combination of attending church and watching television and movies really helped me navigate the trauma of losing him. The same year that my father died, my uncle, Dr. D. J. Williams, started the church Wings of Love, which gave me a positive outlet to process his passing. And it gave me a calling—the preaching I have done since I was fifteen.

Meanwhile, TV programs like *The Cosby Show* and movies like *The Color Purple* really inspired me. Both the church and the arts helped me navigate my personal tragedy, and I became deeply aware of their power to help and to heal. I was led to this epiphany: *Maybe I can use entertainment and faith to help others navigate whatever they're going through.* So that right there was the gift.

And that gift is still giving to me, to this day. It remains the deeper reason behind what I do. This early loss really caused me to figure out who I was. And it motivated what I do in the world. When seen through this lens, it's understandable why I was so committed to my choice to go to the University of Southern California, even when my family had other plans that they believed would be a better option. For me, entertainment wasn't just a cool job. It was a calling, and it came with an intent, a greater purpose, and a sense of having found my true vocation.

Many people don't find this kind of conviction until much later in life, if at all, and so I know I was blessed to gain it so early. And I know it's what has fueled all of my achievements to date.

FIND TREASURE IN TRAGEDY

We don't have to look far to find other examples we can learn from. Comedian and actor Tracy Morgan found treasure in a profound personal challenge—coming back from a devasting multicar accident in 2014. His traumatic brain injury put him into a coma for eight days, and his recovery required extensive physical rehab and cognitive therapy. The accident also caused the death of his good friend and mentor, comedian Jimmy Mack.

Tracy's life has been filled with tribulations of all sorts: a difficult childhood, the loss of his heroin-addicted father to complications from AIDS, and the need to sell crack to survive. Even after he'd achieved major success as a performer, he struggled with alcoholism and drunk-driving arrests before finally getting sober. He'd needed a kidney transplant, survived that, and now lives with diabetes. And he received widespread criticism for an anti-gay joke he made during a comedy set in 2011, which caused him to rethink how he uses the power inherent in his public platform.

All of that was *before* the night the vehicle he was in was struck by a speeding Walmart tractor-trailer, resulting in the horrific crash and its ensuing months of brutal recovery. But after having been blindsided, he fought his way back to health and then found a new role on a TV show that was partly inspired by his life, *The Last O.G.* He has definitely been able to find the silver lining in the unexpected hardship he experienced. As he told Oprah on *Super Soul Sunday*, "I feel like I tapped into humanity and love. . . . And when you look at it, the wreckage, you go, there's no way in the world I was supposed to walk away from it. It's like a second chance."

Can you imagine if Tracy was bitter and only focused on what he had lost? Or if all his thoughts were ones like, *Why did this happen to me?* or *I can't believe I had to go through this.* He would have missed the treasure in adversity. For him, the treasure was a new sense of self and a renewed belief in humanity.

If you have suffered a trauma, lost a beloved family member, or gone through a divorce, obviously the experience is incredibly painful and disorienting. How do you find the treasure in it?

Let's say you recently lost your job. Obsessing on the negatives and only being mad at the fact that it's gone isn't going to bring it back. But looking for the treasure, looking for the hidden blessing, can help you turn a negative in your present into a positive in your future.

That treasure could be greater self-realization. That treasure could be grace. That treasure could be clarity. That treasure could be the recognition that you were going down the wrong path. The key is to ask yourself: *How can I come out of this better than when I went in?* Once you find the answer for yourself, the treasures are always right there.

GET YOUR JOY BACK

UNLOCK THE POWER OF APPRECIATION
AND GET YOUR JOY BACK.

Stop and take an inventory of your life and your obligations, right now—the ones that are left over after you've done the work of setting your expectations. Ask yourself if these obligations are related to what you really want to do, and who you really are, or if they are related to any remaining unset expectations. Ask yourself: *Who am I? Who am I really, not who others think I am but who I am beneath my job title?*

To answer this question, start by taking some quiet time by yourself. Get a notebook and pen. Turn off your phone. Now close your eyes and ask this question. Then write down what you hear or feel. Next, write down the things you're naturally good at, those things you're passionate about, the things most important to you, and what you would do with your life if time or money weren't a factor. Pray and meditate over all that you've written. You will begin to see that you've just created the blueprint for your true self. In order to move in that direction, ask yourself: *What are the biggest changes I must make to be my true self going forward?*

This is about claiming more authority as the creator of the life you are called to live. We know that it's not going to work to outsource our happiness to anyone or anything outside of ourselves, or to assume that we'll be happy when we achieve something in particular. We know better now. And as the great Maya Angelou said, "When you know better, you do better." What we can all practice instead is appreciation.

You may not have the money you want. You may not know where your next job is coming from. You may not be sure how you're going to pay for school. But even if you don't have all that you want, don't allow uncertainty to take you out of a place of appreciation and gratitude. Find something to be grateful for in the present moment.

It's really hard to be angry and appreciative at the same time. So, no matter your circumstances, you can have joy, right now, by practicing appreciation. Anytime you slide toward a bad mood, try this tip to instantly improve how you feel. Stop and do sixty seconds of gratitude. For one full minute, find as many things as you can to be thankful for:

I'm thankful that I'm alive.
I'm thankful that I can see.
I'm thankful that I can hear.

Don't take *anything* for granted. Because when you are appreciative, when you are grateful, you position yourself to receive immediate joy, and you also position yourself for better health.

According to the National Institutes of Health, gratitude has tremendous positive benefits, including fewer signs of heart disease and improved emotional well-being, due to lowered stress levels.

In an article summarizing these findings, Dr. Judith T. Moskowitz, a psychologist at Northwestern University, advises, "We encourage people to try practicing gratitude daily. You can try first thing in the morning or right before you fall asleep, whatever is best for you. . . . By practicing these skills, it will help you cope better with whatever you have to cope with." She goes on to explain: "You don't have to be experiencing major life stress. It also works with the daily stress that we all deal with. Ultimately, it can help you be not just happier but also healthier."

Every big tree starts with a small seed. Plant small seeds of appreciation every day; they will grow into a big life full of joy.

Practicing appreciation applies to all areas of your life. Ask yourself questions like:

- Who do I appreciate most in my life?
- What is the biggest blessing in my life right now?
- What am I most grateful for today?

When you release unset expectations from your relationships and your life overall to focus instead on appreciation, you free up even more gratitude, and you cultivate more joy.

BE FREE TO BE YOU

For the first time in years, maybe since I was that little boy known as "Mr. Perfect," I don't feel any obligation to live up to a certain expectation of who people want DeVon to be. I can see now that I'd been attaching myself to a false sense of who I am, publicly, at the expense of realizing who I really am, personally. There's so much more to me than even I know right this very moment. I can see and feel that now, and that's why I felt called to share the power of this new way of thinking and being with you.

It's really about freedom. You have to choose to be free, and sometimes fight to be free. Free to be everything you were created to be. Free to choose how and where you live, how you worship, who you love. You must build the person you want to be. And in doing so, you will find the recipe for living free.

LIVING FREE IS NOT LIVING WITH NO EXPECTATIONS, BUT LIVING BY YOUR SET EXPECTATIONS.

Learning to live free by setting your expectations for yourself may be very new for you. As a result, you can't be too hard on yourself. And you can't be too hard on anybody else. You've got to give yourself time to learn. You've got to give yourself time to unfold as you're meant to. You've got to give yourself a break. Relax. Don't be too hard on yourself. You can be your own worst critic. Give yourself more credit. You know why? You're doing better than you think.

As you do this work, just because someone expects something of you doesn't make it wrong. If you agree to meet an expectation, fantastic, and if you don't, that's your choice. The key is to make sure that you are living free, that you are choosing the life you want, that you are choosing the life that you're destined to live. Not the one you're obligated to live, not the one you're expected to live, but the one you have chosen and God has created for you.

Let go of pain, let go of resentment, and let go of any energy that you've put into being angry toward anyone in your life. Work through your emotional blocks. Become free.

It's like when you open up your GPS, put in an address, and set your destination. Just as profoundly, your expectations are a direction. When you set them, you set the course for your life. So if you want to move in the right direction, if you want to live free, then you have to use this power daily.

Set your course every day. Set where you want your days to go. Set where you want your weeks to go. Set where you want your months to go. Set where you want your years to go. You'll be shocked at how the more purposefully and realistically you set your course, the more often you not only end up where you wanted but go even further. Not only will you become who you want to be, but you'll become someone even greater. You'll be living with fewer burdens, in the power of who you really are. You'll be more joyful.

Don't be surprised if people in your life start coming up to you and asking, "What's going on with you? What are you doing differently? I've never seen you like this."

You can tell them the truth. All you're doing is working on you. All you're doing is dropping some of this dead weight you've been carrying around your whole life. All you're doing is properly setting your expectations. All you're doing is living free.

ACKNOWLEDGMENTS

I am forever grateful for all the divine and practical assistance I've received to help get this message to the world. I want to thank God and my Lord and Savior Jesus Christ for the opportunity to write and publish yet another book. I'm beyond appreciative. I want to thank my amazing wife, Meagan—you are the love of my life. I want to thank the great Mauro DiPreta—thank you for being a phenomenal leader, editor, and human being; I'm extremely humbled by your belief in me. Thank you to the incomparable team at William Morrow and HarperCollins; my awesome book agent and angel Jan Miller at Dupree Miller; my book confidant and friend Nena Medonia Oshmam; my fearlessly excellent writing collaborator, Sarah Tomlinson—thank you for your help every step of the way; the dynamic Alan Silfen—your photography is art personified, thank you for blessing me yet again with your gift; my wonderful team at Franklin Entertainment—thank you Safiya, Sabrina, Rebecca, Katarina, Karen, Brittany, Jenna, and Alex; and to my mother, Paulette, all my family, my friends, associates, and unbelievable supporters—thank you, and as I always say, "I love you and there's nothing you can do about it."